THE FILIPINO AMERICANS

THE FILIPINO AMERICANS

Jennifer Stern

CHELSEA HOUSE PUBLISHERS
New York Philadelphia

On the cover: Boy Scout troop #284 at the dedication of Benigno Aquino Triangle in Queens, New York, in November 1988.

CHELSEA HOUSE PUBLISHERS
Editor-in-Chief: Nancy Toff
Executive Editor: Remmel T. Nunn
Managing Editor: Karyn Gullen Browne
Copy Chief: Juliann Barbato
Picture Editor: Adrian G. Allen
Art Director: Maria Epes
Manufacturing Manager: Gerald Levine

The Peoples of North America
Senior Editor: Sean Dolan

Staff for THE FILIPINO AMERICANS
Copy Editor: Philip Koslow
Deputy Copy Chief: Nicole Bowen
Editorial Assistant: Elizabeth Nix
Picture Research: PAR/NYC
Assistant Art Director: Loraine Machlin
Senior Designer: Noreen M. Lamb
Production Coordinator: Joseph Romano
Cover Illustration: Paul Biniasz
Banner Design: Hrana L. Janto

3 5 7 9 8 6 4 2

Library of Congress Cataloging-in-Publication Data
Stern, Jennifer.
    The Filipino Americans / Jennifer Stern.
      p.   cm. —(Peoples of North America)
    Summary: Discusses the history, culture, and religion of the Filipinos, factors encouraging their emigration, and their acceptance as an ethnic group in North America.
    1. Filipino Americans–Juvenile literature. [1. Filipino Americans.] I. Title   II. Series.
E184.F4S67   1989
973'.049921—dc19   89-939
ISBN 0-87754-877-3   CIP
      0-7910-0290-X (pbk.)   AC

CONTENTS

THE PEOPLES OF NORTH AMERICA

CHELSEA HOUSE PUBLISHERS

A NATION OF NATIONS

Daniel Patrick Moynihan

The Constitution of the United States begins: "We the People of the United States . . ." Yet, as we know, the United States is not made up of a single group of people. It is made up of many peoples. Immigrants from Europe, Asia, Africa, and Central and South America settled in North America seeking a new life filled with opportunities unavailable in their homeland. Coming from many nations, they forged one nation and made it their own. More than 100 years ago, Walt Whitman expressed this perception of America as a melting pot: "Here is not merely a nation, but a teeming Nation of nations."

Although the ingenuity and acts of courage of these immigrants, our ancestors, shaped the North American way of life, we sometimes take their contributions for granted. This fine series, *The Peoples of North America*, examines the experiences and contributions of the immigrants and how these contributions determined the future of the United States and Canada.

Immigrants did not abandon their ethnic traditions when they reached the shores of North America. Each ethnic group had its own customs and traditions, and each brought different experiences, accomplishments, skills, values, styles of dress, and tastes in food that lingered long after its arrival. Yet this profusion of differences created a singularity, or bond, among the immigrants.

The United States and Canada are unusual in this respect. Whereas religious and ethnic differences have sparked intolerance throughout the rest of the world—from the 17th-century religious wars to the 19th-century nationalist movements in Europe to the near extermination of the Jewish people under Nazi Germany— North Americans have struggled to learn how to respect each other's differences and live in harmony.

Millions of immigrants from scores of homelands brought diversity to our continent. In a mass migration, some 12 million immigrants passed through the waiting rooms of New York's Ellis Island; thousands more came to the West Coast. At first, these immigrants were welcomed because labor was needed to meet the demands of the Industrial Age. Soon, however, the new immigrants faced the prejudice of earlier immigrants who saw them as a burden on the economy. Legislation was passed to limit immigration. The Chinese Exclusion Act of 1882 was among the first laws closing the doors to the promise of America. The Japanese were also effectively excluded by this law. In 1924, Congress set immigration quotas on a country-by-country basis.

Such prejudices might have triggered war, as they did in Europe, but North Americans chose negotiation and compromise instead. This determination to resolve differences peacefully has been the hallmark of the peoples of North America.

The remarkable ability of Americans to live together as one people was seriously threatened by the issue of slavery. It was a symptom of growing intolerance in the world. Thousands of settlers from the British Isles had arrived in the colonies as indentured servants, agreeing to work for a specified number of years on farms or as apprentices in return for passage to America and room and board. When the first Africans arrived in the then-British colonies during the 17th century, some colonists thought that they too should be treated as indentured servants. Eventually, the question of whether the Africans should be viewed as indentured, like the English, or as slaves who could be owned for life, was considered in a Maryland court. The court's calamitous decree held that blacks were slaves bound to lifelong servitude, and so were their children. America went through a time of moral examination and civil war before it finally freed African slaves and their descendants. The principle that all people are created equal had faced its greatest challenge and survived.

Yet the court ruling that set blacks apart from other races fanned flames of discrimination that burned long after slavery was abolished—and that still flicker today. The concept of racism had existed for centuries in countries throughout the world. For instance, when the Manchus conquered China in the 13th century, they decreed that Chinese and Manchus could not intermarry. To impress their superiority on the conquered Chinese, the Manchus ordered all Chinese men to wear their hair in a long braid called a queue.

By the 19th century, some intellectuals took up the banner of racism, citing Charles Darwin. Darwin's scientific studies hypothesized that highly evolved animals were dominant over other animals. Some advocates of this theory applied it to humans, asserting that certain races were more highly evolved than others and thus were superior.

This philosophy served as the basis for a new form of discrimination, not only against nonwhite people but also against various ethnic groups. Asians faced harsh discrimination and were depicted by popular 19th-century newspaper cartoonists as depraved, degenerate, and deficient in intelligence. When the Irish flooded American cities to escape the famine in Ireland, the cartoonists caricatured the typical "Paddy" (a common term for Irish immigrants) as an apelike creature with jutting jaw and sloping forehead.

By the 20th century, racism and ethnic prejudice had given rise to virulent theories of a Northern European master race. When Adolf Hitler came to power in Germany in 1933, he popularized the notion of Aryan supremacy. *Aryan*, a term referring to the Indo-European races, was applied to so-called superior physical characteristics such as blond hair, blue eyes, and delicate facial features. Anyone with darker and heavier features was considered inferior. Buttressed by these theories, the German Nazi state from

1933 to 1945 set out to destroy European Jews, along with Poles, Russians, and other groups considered inferior. It nearly succeeded. Millions of these people were exterminated.

The tragedies brought on by ethnic and racial intolerance throughout the world demonstrate the importance of North America's efforts to create a society free of prejudice and inequality.

A relatively recent example of the New World's desire to resolve ethnic friction nonviolently is the solution the Canadians found to a conflict between two ethnic groups. A long-standing dispute as to whether Canadian culture was properly English or French resurfaced in the mid-1960s, dividing the peoples of the French-speaking Quebec Province from those of the English-speaking provinces. Relations grew tense, then bitter, then violent. The Royal Commission on Bilingualism and Biculturalism was established to study the growing crisis and to propose measures to ease the tensions. As a result of the commission's recommendations, all official documents and statements from the national government's capital at Ottawa are now issued in both French and English, and bilingual education is encouraged.

The year 1980 marked a coming of age for the United States's ethnic heritage. For the first time, the U.S. Census asked people about their ethnic background. Americans chose from more than 100 groups, including French Basque, Spanish Basque, French Canadian, Afro-American, Peruvian, Armenian, Chinese, and Japanese. The ethnic group with the largest response was English (49.6 million). More than 100 million Americans claimed ancestors from the British Isles, which includes England, Ireland, Wales, and Scotland. There were almost as many Germans (49.2 million) as English. The Irish-American population (40.2 million) was third, but the next largest ethnic group, the Afro-Americans, was a distant fourth (21 million). There was a sizable group of French ancestry (13 million), as well as of Italian (12 million). Poles, Dutch, Swedes, Norwegians, and Russians followed. These groups, and other smaller ones, represent the wondrous profusion of ethnic influences in North America.

Canada, too, has learned more about the diversity of its population. Studies conducted during the French/English conflict showed that Canadians were descended from Ukrainians, Germans, Italians, Chinese, Japanese, native Indians, and Eskimos, among others. Canada found it had no ethnic majority, although nearly half of its immigrant population had come from the British Isles. Canada, like the United States, is a land of immigrants for whom mutual tolerance is a matter of reason as well as principle.

The people of North America are the descendants of one of the greatest migrations in history. And that migration is not over. Koreans, Vietnamese, Nicaraguans, Cubans, and many others are heading for the shores of North America in large numbers. This mix of cultures shapes every aspect of our lives. To understand ourselves, we must know something about our diverse ethnic ancestry. Nothing so defines the North American nations as the motto on the Great Seal of the United States: *E Pluribus Unum*— Out of Many, One.

Some of the earliest Filipino immigrants worked on Hawaii's pineapple plantations. Filipinos came seeking jobs and a better way of life than they had known at home; many found unending toil, poverty, and racial discrimination instead.

AN ONGOING STORY

Filipinos have been coming to the United States in significant numbers from their island nation in the southwest Pacific Ocean since the early 1900s. Yet with the exception of a brief period during the late 1920s and early 1930s—coinciding roughly with the onset of the Great Depression—when Filipino immigrants found themselves the targets of violent racial attacks, Filipinos have remained an essentially overlooked minority in the United States. That has changed in recent years. The Immigration Act of 1965 opened a new era in Filipino immigration. With the removal of the barriers that had effectively barred their entry since the 1930s, Filipinos came to this country in record numbers. The period from 1965 to the present has witnessed a great wave of Filipino immigration. In just the first 10 years following the passage of the 1965 Immigration Act, more than 250,000 Filipinos emigrated to the United States. The drama surrounding the overthrow of the Philipines's dictatorial president, Ferdinand Marcos, by Corazon Aquino in 1986 also did much to focus the attention of Americans on the Philippines and their people. There are currently more than 1 million Americans of Filipino

Maria Abastilla Beltran (left) was one of the comparatively small number of Pinays (female Filipino immigrants) who came to the United States before World War II.

descent, and next to Mexicans, Filipinos are the fastest growing immigrant group in the United States.

The new generation of Filipino Americans differs considerably from those who came in the first three decades of this century. For the most part, the new immigrants were educated professionals seeking the greater economic opportunities available to them in the United States. More than two-thirds of them qualified for entry under the 1965 legislation as "professional, technical, and kindred workers." Many were doctors, nurses, pharmacists, and dentists, trained in American-style schools, fluent in English. They usually came with their family and intended to stay permanently in the United States. Most settled in urban areas, predominantly on the West Coast, although New York City and Chicago also feature sizable Filipino communities.

Their earlier counterparts lacked the education and training required to achieve immediate success in the New World, and they arrived without the language skills that would have helped them assimilate. Virtually all were young men, under the age of 30, peasants who exchanged impoverished lives as tenant farmers for what they hoped would be short stints as contract laborers on Hawaii's sugarcane plantations or as migrant laborers in California's fruit and vegetable fields. Few expected their stay to be permanent; most hoped to save enough money to return to their homeland and purchase their own tract of land.

This first wave of Filipino immigrants received a much harsher welcome than would the later generation. Working hours were long—60 to 70 hours a week. Wages were low—one or two dollars a day. Home was most likely the barracklike dwellings provided by the Hawaiian plantation owners or the rude shacks of a California migrant labor camp. One hundred and thirteen thousand Filipinos immigrated to Hawaii between 1909 and 1931, whereas slightly more than 50,000 made their way to the U.S. mainland during that same period, the great majority of them to California. As their numbers grew, the Asian immigrants earned the enmity of other Americans, who worried that the newcomers would take away jobs, even though few Americans were willing to perform the sort of backbreaking, low-paying agricultural labor the Filipinos provided. Hostility increased when millions of Americans became unemployed during the Great Depression. Economic fears and racism went hand in hand. Legislation forbade Filipinos from marrying whites, becoming citizens, or from practicing various professions, and immigrants became the target for mob violence.

Hard times drove many of the first wave of Filipino immigrants to return to their homeland, but thousands of others persevered. Filipino-American sugarcane workers in Hawaii began organizing into unions and demanding higher wages and better working conditions in the 1930s. By 1950 their determination had made Hawaiian plantation workers the highest paid agricultural laborers in the world. Filipino Americans also played a prominent role in the labor movement in California, where they ardently supported the attempts of Cesar Chavez's United Farm Workers to obtain better treatment for the state's agricultural laborers. Filipinos were declared eligible to become U.S. citizens in 1946; two years later the miscegenation laws that prohibited them from marrying whites were declared unconstitutional. The struggle for equality by the first generation of Filipino immigrants helped make the United States a more hospitable nation for the hundreds of thousands of their compatriots who came later, just as the contributions of the new generations of Filipino Americans help create a more vibrant society for their descendants and all Americans.

THE PHILIPPINES: ORIGINS TO INDEPENDENCE

The nation known as the Republic of the Philippines consists of more than 7,100 islands located about 500 miles off the southeast coast of Asia. Together the islands have a land mass of 115,651 square miles—approximately the size of the state of Arizona. Most of the islands are tiny—only 462 measure more than a square mile—and fewer than 1,000 are inhabited. The two largest are Mindanao, in the south, and Luzon, in the north, which together make up about 67 percent of the Philippines's land area. Between the two largest islands are a cluster of smaller ones, known collectively as the Visayans, which are the Philippines's most densely populated regions. The nation's capital and largest city, Manila, is situated on Luzon. Mindanao is the historical center of the religion of Islam in the Philippines. Filipino Muslims, known as Moros, still live in the southern regions of Mindanao and the islands to the southwest known as the Sulu archipelago, but the overwhelming majority of the population, about 80 percent, is Roman

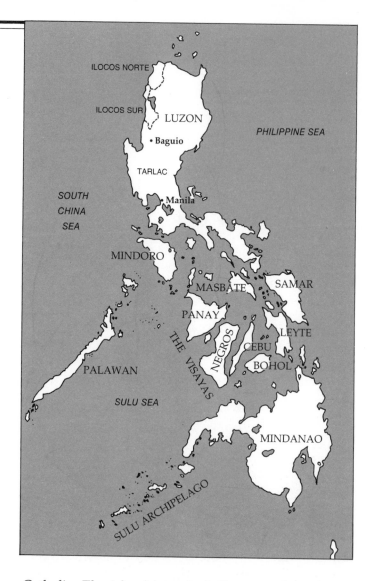

Catholic. The islands' tropical climate and fertile soil enable a wide variety of crops to be grown there. Although much industrialization has occurred since World War II, agriculture is still the lifeblood of the economy. Rice, corn, coconuts, tobacco, sugarcane, coffee, and pineapples are the most important cash crops. The Philippines are heavily forested, and timber, particularly mahogany, is one of the nation's most important exports.

The islands support a rapidly growing population. In 1980 the count was almost 48 million; at the current rate of growth that figure will double by the year 2007. The populace is divided into many different groups. There are 8 or 9 predominant languages in the Philippines, with some 80 different dialects. The Philippines have been an independent nation only since 1946; its citizens are as likely to define themselves by the region they come from and the language they speak as they are as Filipinos. The three largest groups are the Visayans, who inhabit the central islands; the Tagalogs, who live mainly on the island of Luzon, in and around Manila; and the Ilocanos, who occupy the northwest provinces of Luzon. The cultural influence of the Spanish, who ruled the Philippines as a colony for more than 300 years, is seen most clearly among the Visayans, the largest group. The Tagalogs are often held to be the most learned of the Filipinos. A variant of their language, known as Pilipino (pronounced *Filipino*), is one of the nation's three official languages, along with English and Spanish. The third largest

Visayan women carry coconut sap to market on the island of Cebu in the early days of the 20th century. Visayans occupy the central islands of the Philippines.

group, the Ilocanos, constituted the majority of the earliest wave of Filipino immigrants to the United States.

In the Beginning

The different Filipino peoples today are the descendants of the many groups who, over thousands of years, came to the Philippines for settlement or conquest. Anthropologists believe humans first arrived in the Philippines more than 250,000 years ago, during the Ice Age, over land bridges that then connected China and the islands. These first inhabitants lived in relative isolation on the islands for thousands of years. They developed sophisticated farming techniques to take advantage of the fertile soil and temperate climate, and they became accomplished sailors, which enabled them to bring jade and other prized materials from China and other nearby lands.

Other peoples began to arrive on the islands in about 25,000 B.C. One of the first was a group the Spaniards called the Negritos, or "Little People," because they are small—less than five feet tall—and dark skinned. Hunters and gatherers, they established

A Tagalog family, photographed in the late 1890s. Tagalogs are the most numerous of the various Filipino peoples.

Contemporary descendants of the Negritos, the aboriginal settlers of the Philippines. Today the Negritos live primarily in the mountainous regions of the Philippines and are as likely to practice agriculture as their traditional hunting and gathering.

themselves in the mountains of Mindanao and nearby Palawan, where their descendants still live in relative isolation from the rest of Filipino society. Today, less than one percent of the Filipino populace are Negritos.

The most important of the early groups that settled the Philippines were the Malays, who migrated from the nearby Malaysian peninsula and Indonesia from the 3rd through the 14th centuries. Distinguished physically by their brown skin, medium height, and straight black hair, the Malays are the ancestors of more than a third of the Filipinos today. They brought with them their laws, language, alphabet, and folklore, as well as their religious practices, which centered on the worship of ancestral spirits. Active traders, the Malays carried on commerce with Indian, Chinese, and Middle Eastern merchants. The Philippines became an active trading area, in the process absorbing cultural influences from their business partners, most notably the religion of Islam, which was introduced by Malay traders and settlers during the 14th century.

The Spanish

It was the Europeans who would prove to be the greatest cultural influence on the Philippines during the Middle Ages. By the end of the 15th century, Spain was busy establishing the colonies in the New World

Filipino Muslims are known as Moros. Some speak Arabic; a large number live on the southern island of Mindanao. Moros were among the last Filipinos to submit to U.S. rule.

that would give it a vast and wealthy empire. Despite their success in the Americas, Spain's monarchs and adventurous mariners had not lost sight of the goal that had inspired Columbus's voyages—the discovery of a sea route to Asia. The European nations had long been eager to establish trading posts and colonies in the Far East in order to avail themselves of the spices and precious metals to be found there and to convert the native inhabitants to Christianity.

In 1521 Ferdinand Magellan, a Portuguese ship captain who was sailing for the Spanish, landed in the Philippines after sailing west from Spain, then south around the tip of South America. Although Magellan had not been searching specifically for the Philippines—his original destination had been the Moluccas, known also as the Spice Islands—his arrival there on March 17 made him the first to prove Columbus's theory that one could reach the East by sailing west. Magellan was able to befriend a powerful chief on Cebu, one of the Visayan islands, whose people swore fealty to the king of Spain and promised to convert to Christianity, but his reception elsewhere was less warm. While attempting to land on the island of Mactan, where the inhabitants were at war with the Cebu chieftain, Magellan was slain, as were many of his men. The 3 Spanish ships that remained—5 had left Spain in 1519—continued west, but only 1, with just 18 men aboard, made it safely back to Spain.

Magellan's success piqued the interest of Spain's monarch, Charles I, who dispatched three expeditions there and to the Spice Islands from 1525 to 1536. It was the commander of the third voyage, Rui Lopez de Villalobos, who dubbed the islands the Philippines, in honor of the king's son and heir, Philip, who would rule Spain from 1556 to 1598. The Spice Islands continued to attract most of Spain's attention for several decades, but in 1565 the Spanish began efforts to colonize the Philippines. Six years later they conquered the settlement of Manila and proclaimed it to be the capital of the new colony. Much of the work of colonization was performed by Catholic missionaries who were members of the Augustinian, Franciscan, Dominican, and Jesuit religious orders. The government of Spain subsidized the work of the missionaries in exchange for the right to make appointments to fill important

This 16th-century engraving portrays the fantastic creatures and sights that superstitious Europeans believed Magellan would encounter on his voyage around the world.

The Spanish monarch Philip II, for whom the Philippines was named, as portrayed by the Venetian painter Tintoretto, one of the greatest artists of the Italian Renaissance.

church posts. The missionaries built schools and settlements; in many cases they functioned as the civil authorities for the Spanish government. As the Spanish extended their influence steadily southward from Manila, practically the entire population was converted to Christianity, with the exception of the Muslims of Mindanao and Sulu.

The Spanish solidified their control of the Philippines with the help of two systems of forced labor that they had used with success in their American colonies. The *encomienda* gave an individual Spaniard control over a number of Filipinos, who were required to work for him in exchange for his providing them with food, shelter, and protection. In practice, the encomienda functioned as little more than slavery. The *repartimiento* was used by Spaniards to draft Filipinos for labor on public works, usually shipyards and lumber factories.

Although the Spanish came to the Philippines with visions of great wealth, it took several centuries for the colony to become economically self-sufficient. Until the 19th century, its primary value to the Spanish was as a middleman in the China to Mexico trade. Chinese traders had silks, spices, porcelain, perfumes, and other goods that were coveted in Mexico. The Chinese in turn greatly desired Mexican silver, but only the Spanish, by virtue of their control of the Philippines and possession of ships capable of making the ocean crossing, were in the position to carry on commerce between the two lands. Chinese junks carried their goods to Manila, where they were snapped up by Spanish merchants. Spanish galleons then carried the lucrative cargo across the Pacific to Mexico, where it was exchanged for silver. The trade proved extremely profitable for the Spanish.

Profits for the Spanish did not mean better lives for their Filipino subjects. The Spanish, the church, and a few *mestizos* (people with mixed Filipino and Spanish blood) owned almost all the land. Most Filipinos were forced to work as agricultural laborers; their wages were small or nonexistent. There was no public school system until 1863, and Filipinos were not allowed to attend the universities established by the Spanish until the end of the 17th century. Even then, very few Fili-

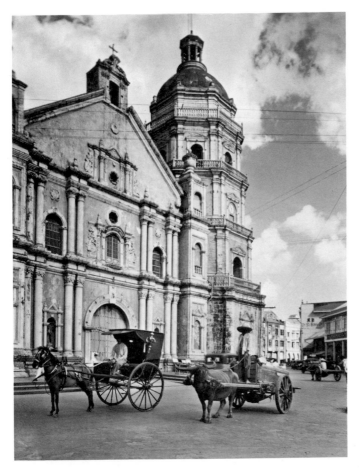

The Cathedral of Manila, seen here in a photograph from the late 1920s, is an example of the Spanish-style architecture that could once be found in the Philippine capital. Much of the old Spanish section of the city, known as the Intramuros, was destroyed during World War II.

pinos were admitted. Although some Filipinos achieved success as planters, merchants, and low-level civil servants, most of the islands' inhabitants found Spanish rule extremely oppressive.

By the middle of the 19th century, the Filipinos had attempted more than 100 revolts against the Spanish. As British and U.S. influence in the Philippines increased, the Spanish repression grew harsher, culminating in the execution of 3 Filipino priests in 1872 following a revolt by 200 Filipino soldiers against their Spanish officers.

The opposition movement was led by a group of young Filipinos, many of them educated in Spain, known as the propagandists. Its most prominent leader was José Protasio Rizal, who had been trained in Spain as a physician. In 1886 Rizal published a novel, *Noli Me Tangere (Touch Me Not)*, that harshly attacked Spanish rule in the Philippines. The book caused a sensation, and the Spanish exiled Rizal from his homeland. In an essay written three years later, Rizal spoke of how the excesses of Spanish rule were uniting the Filipino masses and warned that unless reforms occurred quickly, a conflagration was inevitable:

> [I]f the complaints and demands of the Filipino people are always to meet with the invariable No recommended by the vested interests that batten on the depressed condition of the masses . . .

José Rizal—physician, novelist, poet, and the Philippines's greatest national hero.

if, in short, we are to continue under the policy, only too successful, of alienating the affections of the natives, or heaping insult and ingratitude on their supposed lack of feeling, then we can confidently affirm that in a few years, the present [untroubled] state of affairs will change completely.

Rizal's second novel protesting the inequities of Spanish rule, *El Filibusterismo (Filibustering)*, appeared in 1891, at the same time he was organizing the Liga Filipina, which operated out of Hong Kong and was devoted to bringing about peaceful reform, especially land redistribution, in the Philippines. When Rizal returned to Manila in 1892, he was arrested and banished to the island of Mindanao for four years. The unrest in the Philippines grew stronger, exacerbated by several bad harvests. Meanwhile, on the island of Luzon, a warehouse worker named Andrés Bonifacio had organized a secret revolutionary organization known as the Katipunan, or the Supreme Worshipful Association of the Sons of the People. Made up almost exclusively of Tagalogs, its membership grew to more than 100,000 by 1896. On August 26 of that year, the revolt began. Spain immediately sent reinforcements for its rather small garrison in the Philippines. Initially, the fighting was heaviest in central and southern Luzon, where Emilio Aguinaldo came to prominence as the rebels' most skillful general and, over time, as the rebellion's leader. Hostilities died down after a couple of months, but the arrest and subsequent execution of Rizal incited armed opposition in all parts of the country. December 30, the date of Rizal's execution, is still celebrated by Filipinos as a national holiday.

After a year of fighting the rebels signed a truce with the Spanish, and Aguinaldo went into exile in Hong Kong. But in February 1898 war between the United States and Spain broke out over the United States's determination to aid Cuban rebels in their struggle for independence against Spanish rule. A U.S. fleet under Admiral George Dewey arrived in Manila and destroyed Spanish ships anchored there, and U.S. troops moved into Manila.

Liberation and Betrayal

Dewey encouraged Aguinaldo to resume his rebellion, and the Filipino leader, believing that the United States also intended to help the Philippines gain its independence, eagerly complied. Aguinaldo's forces liberated several towns south of Manila and declared the Philippines an independent nation. Over the next six months, the Filipinos organized a constitutional government with Aguinaldo as president.

Hostilities between the United States and Spain had ended, but at the peace talks held in Paris beginning in October 1898 the U.S. negotiators stunned the Filipinos by demanding that Spain cede the islands to the United States. Victory over Spain had given the United States the beginnings of an empire in the Pacific—it now also controlled Guam and other Pacific islands formerly held by the Spanish—and imperialists in the Congress were pressing President William McKinley to hold on to the Philippines for use as a military base and a point from which to pursue profitable trade relations with China. McKinley concurred, disguising U.S. opportunism by proclaiming that the United States was merely acting in the best interests of the Filipinos, who were not yet ready for independence. He told a group of Methodist clergymen who visited the White House:

> I walked the floor of the White House, night after night until midnight; and I am not afraid to tell you, gentlemen, that I went down on my knees

On the morning of May 1, 1898, an American fleet under Admiral Dewey engaged 10 Spanish ships in combat in Manila Bay. All of the Spanish ships were destroyed; the American victory marked the beginning of the end of Spanish rule in the Philippines.

and prayed . . . for guidance. . . . And one night late it came to me . . . that there was nothing left for us to do but to take them all, and to educate the Filipinos, and uplift and civilize and Christianize them, and by God's grace do the very best we could for them, as our fellow men.

The Filipinos did not agree with McKinley's racist assumption that they were incapable of governing themselves without American assistance. They had no desire to exchange one colonial overlord for another, and they regarded the U.S. action as a betrayal. Fighting between U.S. troops stationed in Manila and Aguinaldo's forces broke out on February 4, 1899. Over the next several years more than 100,000 Filipinos lost their lives fighting U.S. troops, and another 100,000 may have died as a result of the devastation and hardship caused by the war. Organized resistance ended after Aguinaldo's capture in 1901, although sporadic opposition occurred for several years, particularly among the Moros of Mindanao and the southern islands.

The American decision to rule the Philippines as a colonial possession rather than grant it independence after the defeat of Spain enraged Filipinos. During the insurrection that followed, much of the native quarter of Manila was burned to the ground.

A New Master

U.S. rule had as its purpose the preparation of the Philippines for self-government. William Howard Taft, who in 1908 would become president of the United States, became the first American governor of the Philippines in 1901. He was aided by an appointed commission consisting of both Americans and Filipinos.

Beginning in 1907, Filipinos had the right to elect members to a legislative assembly. Nine years later, the assembly was joined by an elected senate, which replaced the appointed commission. Bills passed by the legislature and approved by the governor became law, although monetary, foreign, and military policy for the Philippines was determined by the U.S. president and Congress, in which Filipinos were not represented. The Nacionalista party, which advocated Philippine independence, usually won most of the seats in the legislature. Sergio Osmeña and Manuel Quezon y Molina were its two most important leaders.

Perhaps the greatest benefit of U.S. rule in the Philippines was the establishment of an American-style system of public education. Public schools, staffed initially by American teachers, were established throughout the nation. Lessons were taught in English, which was soon made an official language. That all Filipinos were taught English made it easier for them to communicate with one another, although the traditional languages were still used. Most Filipinos had disliked the church-affiliated schools established by the Spanish, and the American schools proved very popular. Within a short time, American-trained Filipino teachers began taking their place in the classroom. The American emphasis on education was also responsible for bringing some of the first Philippine immigrants to the United States. Under a plan proposed by Taft, hundreds of Filipino students, known as *pensionados*, were awarded scholarships to American universities for study in such fields as medicine, engineering, and education. It was hoped that on their return to the Philippines they would act as advocates of American-style democracy and help prepare their countrymen for the transition to independence.

The Americans also succeeded in diminishing the influence of the church. Church and state were kept strictly separate, and clerics were stripped of their civil authority. The friar lands—huge agricultural estates whose ownership by the church had long been a source of irritation to Filipino nationalists—were broken up and redistributed. Great inroads were made in health education and in the control of tropical diseases.

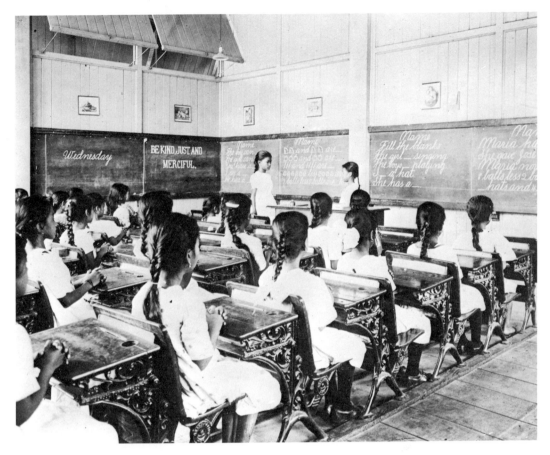

Schools conducted educational campaigns regarding sanitation and other hygiene issues. Attempts were made to vaccinate all Filipinos against smallpox, although this and other American health initiatives ran into opposition because they violated traditional customs.

Much of the Philippines's transportation system was developed under American rule. American dollars helped fund the construction of roads, bridges, and railroads. The improved transportation made it easier for Filipino agricultural products to reach market, a goal that became increasingly important as American companies began earning profits from such imported Filipino products as sugar, copra (dried coconut), abaca, and tobacco. Although the Americans had ini-

During the 48 years of American rule over the Philippines, a nationwide public education program was established. Lessons were conducted in English, which became the most commonly spoken language of the Philippines. It remains one of the island nation's three official languages.

Filipinos building a road through the rugged mountains of northern Luzon in 1924. Under American rule, much highway construction took place in the Philippines.

tially attempted land redistribution, American agricultural concerns operating in the Philippines found large estates, manned by landless tenant farmers, to be more profitable than other methods of production. Rural poverty continued to be the Philippines's greatest problem during the years of U.S. rule.

The continued deprivation in their homeland and the economic opportunity seemingly available in the United States convinced a number of Filipinos to emigrate at this time. Immigration to the United States was relatively easy because as inhabitants of a U.S. possession, Filipinos carried U.S. passports and were able to enter and exit the United States freely. Thus, Filipinos were unaffected by legislation in the early 1920s that established quotas for the number of members of each immigrant group allowed to legally enter the United States. More than 150,000 Filipinos immigrated to the United States between 1900 and 1934. Most of them settled in California or Hawaii, which at the time was a U.S. territory and not yet a state.

This changed in 1934, when the U.S. Congress passed the Tydings-McDuffie Act, which gave the Philippines commonwealth status for the next 10 years. Although some Filipino nationalists hailed the legislation as a step on the road to independence, the act had been inspired in large part by anti-Filipino sentiment in the United States. With the onset of the Great Depression, many Americans believed that unemployment could be eased by eliminating immigrant labor, and the racial prejudice to which Filipinos had long been subjected boiled over in several violent incidents. The Tydings-McDuffie Act allowed only 50 Filipinos per year to enter the United States. Legislators attempted not only to end Filipino immigration but to secure the removal of Filipinos already in the country. The Repatriation Act of 1935 provided free transportation back to the Philippines for those immigrants who were ready to leave. The Tydings-McDuffie Act also affected commerce between the Philippines and the United States. Although previously, Filipino exports were allowed into the United States without duties, under the Tydings-McDuffie Act, Philippine goods sold in the United States were subject to ever-increasing tariffs. American goods, however, could still be brought into the Philippines without the payment of import taxes.

Smoke rises from the flaming hulks of U.S. vessels at the navy yard in Cavite, the Philippines, following a Japanese bombing raid there on December 12, 1941. The Philippines was the site of ferocious fighting during World War II.

On October 23, 1944, U.S. general Douglas MacArthur (center, in dark glasses) announced that he was turning over the government of the Philippines to its president-in-exile, Sergio Osmeña, but months of combat lay ahead before the Philippines would be freed of its Japanese invaders.

The 1930s witnessed the rise of Japan as a power in Asia. The Japanese surprise attack on the U.S. military base at Pearl Harbor, Hawaii, early in the morning on December 7, 1941, was followed by a bombing raid on Clark Field in the Philippines hours later. When the Japanese invaded the Philippines several days later, the U.S. commander, General Douglas MacArthur, withdrew his comparatively small force to a defensive position on the Bataan peninsula, due west from Manila. Despite heroic resistance by the Filipinos, the Japanese captured Manila and advanced steadily southward. In February 1942, MacArthur, vowing to someday return, left the Philippines to take charge of the Allied war effort in the Pacific. He was accompanied by Manuel Quezon y Molina, who had been elected president of the commonwealth in 1935. Que-

zon established a Filipino government-in-exile in Washington, D.C. The U.S. forces on Bataan and the nearby island of Corregidor held on for more than another year before surrendering. The Japanese occupation, which lasted until several months after MacArthur's return in October 1944 at the head of a triumphant American fighting force, was uncommonly harsh. More than 1 million Filipinos perished during that period, and Manila was left utterly devastated.

Independence

The Philippines finally achieved its independence on July 4, 1946. Recognizing its former dependent's need for economic aid in order to rebuild its shattered economy, the United States appropriated $620 million for postwar reconstruction, but the money came with a few strings attached. The United States received 99-year leases on Philippine military bases, and the island nation's constitution was amended to give U.S. businesses and industries certain rights to the Philippines' natural resources. In the eyes of the U.S. Immigration and Naturalization Service, with independence the Philippines achieved the same status under the 1920s immigration law as any other Asian country, which meant that not more than 100 Filipinos were allowed to immigrate to the United States each year. This strict quota was not lifted until President Lyndon Johnson signed a new immigration act in 1965, opening the floodgates for a new generation of Filipino immigrants.

CONSTITUCION Y ESTATUTOS

DE LA

Sociedad de Beneficencia

DE LOS

Hispano Filipinos

DE

NUEVA ORLEANS.

Fundada el 24 de Julio de 1870, y aprobada por los
Miembros activos de la Sociedad.

NUEVA ORLEANS,

Imprenta de M. Capo, Calle Decatur No. 133.

1895.

FILIPINO IMMIGRATION: THE FIRST WAVE

The very first Filipinos to journey to America came long before the United States was even a country. They were unwilling sailors, drafted into seagoing service by the Spanish, who crossed the Pacific Ocean on the trade route between Manila and Acapulco as early as 1565. They were often treated badly, and many of them jumped ship in Mexico. Some settled there, where they easily fit in because they spoke Spanish, but others—perhaps a few hundred in number—made their way to Louisiana by ship or mule train. There they settled in the marshes and bayous outside New Orleans, building villages of houses on stilts. Known to themselves and others as Manilamen, these settlers married local women and made their living as fishermen. The very first Filipino community organization in the United States, the Sociedad de Beneficencia de los Hispano Filipinos de Nuevo Orleans, was founded in Louisiana in 1870. A few other Filipinos appear in American history before the onset of the first wave of Filipino immigration. Anthony Miranda, who in 1781 was one of the 46 founders of the city of Los Angeles, was reportedly of Filipino descent. Small groups of Filipino sailors settled in Hawaii and Alaska. Yet Filipinos did not come to this country in large numbers until the early days of the 20th century and the beginnings of U.S. rule over their nation.

A Small Part of the Great Wave

The early 1900s was the period of heaviest immigration to the United States and Canada from all parts of the world. The decade from 1901 to 1910 brought more immigrants than any other: 8,790,000 individuals made the trip to America at that time. The next 10 years brought 5,740,000 settlers to America's shores. The great majority of the immigrants were eastern and southern Europeans—Italians, Greeks, Ukrainians, Slovaks, Serbians, Russian Jews, Croatians, Hungarians, and others. The slightly more than 150,000 Filipinos who immigrated to the United States during the first two decades of the 20th century represented just a small portion of the total number of newcomers, but even so, they alarmed more established Americans, many of whom were the descendants of earlier immigrants. Anti-Asian prejudice had long been rampant in the United States, as reflected in the various Oriental exclusion acts that had closed the doors to Chinese immigration beginning in the 1880s and the Immigration Act of 1924, which effectively barred all other Asians, particularly the Japanese.

The 1924 legislation was not directed only at Asians; it sprang from the belief that the new immigrants were racially inferior to their predecessors from northern and western Europe and less suited to the American way of life. Whereas in the early years of the century an average of 850,000 immigrants entered the United States each year, the 1924 Immigration Act limited that number to a maximum of 165,000. By setting the quota for the number of individuals eligible to enter from each nation at two percent of the foreign-born of that nationality recorded in the 1890 census, Congress ensured that the great majority of those allowed to enter would be of northern and western

Cartoonist Thomas Nast expressed American fears about the dangers posed by Chinese labor in this 1880s drawing. Concern that Americans would lose jobs to immigrants led to a number of anti-Asian immigration acts, but as citizens of an American possession Filipinos were exempt from exclusionary legislation.

European stock, as the heaviest immigration of those groups—German, British, Irish, and others—had occurred prior to 1890. A provision that prohibited all foreigners ineligible for citizenship from entering guaranteed that no Asians—particularly Japanese, at whom it was directed—would be allowed to enter because the Naturalization Act of 1790, which restricted citizenship to "free white persons," had long been used to deny Asians citizenship. (An 1870 amendment to the act extended citizenship to blacks.) The 1924 act did not apply to Filipinos, who were fortunate in that as American nationals they were entitled to U.S. passports and could enter and leave the country freely, although once here they were often subjected to racial prejudice and sometimes violence. Still, except for those few who had served three years in either the navy or the marines during World War I, Filipinos were ineligible for U.S. citizenship, and they possessed an ambiguous legal status. They were not entitled to bear arms or to a trial by jury. Although they were allowed to take federal civil service exams, the licensing boards of most states prohibited them from practicing many professions. Because they were not citizens, during the hard times of the Great Depression, Filipino Americans did not qualify for the benefits available under the social programs of the New Deal.

The Pensionados

Despite the widespread poverty in their homeland and the opportunity for unrestricted entrance, Filipinos did not clamor to emigrate. Filipino immigration began very slowly. The first groups to come had to be invited or coaxed, and most of those who came in the early 20th century did not intend to stay.

The first Filipino immigrants came at the invitation of the U.S. government, beginning in 1903. These young men and women—some of the brightest students in the Philippines—were sent to this country to finish their education in American universities. Known as pensionados, because their education was paid for by the U.S. government, the students lived with American families while they pursued their studies in such fields as education, engineering, agriculture, and medicine. The pensionados attended a total of 47 different U.S. schools. The purpose of the program was to teach the young Filipinos—considered by the U.S. government to be "trainees in democracy"—those skills that would be most useful in developing their own country. About 500 young Filipinos participated in the pensionado program, and more than 200 of them received their college degrees or completed advanced training. By 1910, all of them had returned home, where, despite some initial mistrust and jealously among other Filipinos, many became leaders in their communities.

Although the pensionados were few in number, they paved the way for thousands of Filipino students who came to the United States in later years. These young men and women did not receive scholarships, as the pensionados had, but they judged the expense of an American education well worth it. For young Filipinos, the United States was the logical place to pursue an education in science, social sciences, or technological fields, because educational opportunities in the Philippines were limited either to the University of the Philippines, started by the Americans in 1908, or to older Philippine colleges controlled by the Roman Catholic church, which placed little emphasis on scientific training. Between 1910 and 1938, some 14,000 Filipinos enrolled in U.S. schools. Despite the high cost of living in the United States and of university tuition, many successfully completed their studies. Most returned to the Philippines when they were through.

The Pinoys

The great majority of Filipino immigrants to the United States during the early 20th century came in search of work, not education. Most were young men under the age of 30. They called themselves Pinoys, or, in the case of the few female immigrants, Pinays. Almost all settled in Hawaii or on the West Coast, particularly California.

Hawaii and California were the destinations of most Pinoys because both states were among the United States's leading sources of agricultural products. Hawaii's most important products were sugarcane and pineapples; California's fertile valleys and temperate climate were conducive to the cultivation of lettuce, sugar beets, asparagus, celery, garlic, grapes, and other crops. For years the growers in both places had relied on immigrant labor, particularly Oriental immigrants, to plant their fields and harvest their crops. Such jobs were low paying and physically exhausting, but for many immigrants the wages and work were better than anything available to them in the homeland. In the 1800s, Chinese and Japanese had filled most of the jobs as agricultural workers in Hawaii and California, but with the passage of the various laws aimed at excluding Orientals from the United States, that labor pool dwindled.

Filipinos in Hawaii

With a pressing need for a new source of labor, growers began to look to the Philippines, which was not affected by the new immigration legislation. Beginning in 1906, representatives of the Hawaiian Sugar Plant-

Filipinos Gregorio Matutino and Agustin Lelipa Matutino came to Hawaii in 1959 seeking jobs on a sugar plantation. Filipinos had provided the bulk of Hawaii's agricultural labor needs since the early decades of the 20th century.

Unlike the majority of their eastern European counterparts, who labored in mills, factories, and mines, most Filipino immigrants worked outside under a hot sun, but their jobs were no less exhausting.

ers' Association (HSPA) began traveling to the Philippines in order to encourage young Filipino men to join. The growers' agents offered good wages and decent housing to those Filipinos willing to enlist for work on the sugarcane plantations. Although the wages were extremely low by American standards, they sounded high to Filipinos—many of them jobless and from poor families—accustomed to a much less expensive standard of living than they would find in America. Thousands of young Filipino men signed three-year contracts with the HSPA that guaranteed free passage to Hawaii, wages, housing, water, fuel, and medical attention. Others booked passage for Hawaii and California on their own, certain that they would be able to find work in the fields when they arrived. Nearly all intended to remain in Hawaii or California only until they had earned and saved enough money to buy some land at home.

The first of the Filipino workers under contract to the HSPA arrived in Hawaii on December 20, 1906. They were 15 in number, including a 56-year-old father, Simplicio Gironella, and his 4 sons, aged 14 to 23. The members of the HSPA were more than satisfied with the work habits of these Pinoys and the others who followed over the next few years, and they began to recruit even more aggressively in the Philippines. More than 4,000 young Filipino men came to the Hawaiian islands under contract to the HSPA in 1910. About 2,000 Filipinos came to Hawaii each year over the next decade, so that by 1920 there were more than 21,000 Filipinos, almost all of them men, living and working on the territory's sugar plantations. That number increased to 63,000 by the early 1930s, before the Tydings-McDuffie Act and the Great Depression all but halted Filipino immigration. Most of these immigrants were Ilocanos, from the Ilocos provinces of northwest Luzon. The growers believed the Ilocanos to be better workers than other Filipinos because they were taller and stronger and supposedly better accustomed to agricultural life and work than the Tagalogs, who the growers believed were too urban, or the Visayans, who the growers regarded as too easygoing to make good laborers. In truth, the growers had more luck recruiting in the Ilocos provinces because the region was poorer and more heavily populated than other areas of the Philippines. With their opportunities quite limited at home, many Ilocano young men—some of them no more than teenagers—were quite willing to travel elsewhere for work.

A Hard Life

By 1926, the desire of Filipinos to immigrate to Hawaii was so great that sugarcane growers no longer found it necessary to provide such inducements as medical coverage and guaranteed passage back to the Philippines upon completion of a contract. Many families in the *barrios*, or villages, of the Philippines had benefited from money sent back by immigrants, and Hawaiianos, as Ilocanos who returned to their home provinces were called, were highly regarded in their communities. Many Hawaiianos were able to purchase land for themselves and their relatives upon their return. But life on the sugar plantations was far from easy, although working conditions were not that much different from those in other American agricultural industries. The growing and harvesting season lasted eight or nine months. Filipinos planted, cultivated, and harvested the sugarcane, but the most taxing work was cutting the cane, which could grow from 8 to 24 feet tall. The cane was cut with a machete, and it was hot and dirty work, particularly because a field would be burned a day before harvesting was to begin to make the cutting easier. It took only a few hours' cutting before the men were covered with soot and ashes. Once the cane was cut, the workers loaded it onto heavy carts that ran on temporary tracks, laid by the Filipinos, from the fields to the sugar mills. In the mills, which were also manned by Filipino immigrants, the cane was pressed and rinsed until it yielded a sugary solution, which was then dried and distilled until it became sugar. During the off-season, the Filipino laborers worked at a variety of other jobs on the plantations.

A typical work week lasted 6 days, 10 hours a day. Work began at 6:00 A.M., which meant the workers had to be up and ready by 5:00 to meet the trucks that took them out to the fields. The work was intensely physical, and they had to be strong and fit enough to exert themselves all day in the hot Hawaiian sun. According to H. Brett Melendy, author of *Asians in America*, "Filipinos who later wrote or talked about their experiences agreed that their work in Hawaii was the hardest they had ever undertaken." In 1915, the average male worker in both the fields and the mills received $1 a day; by 1925 that figure had risen to between $2.25 and $2.50 a day, although most planters were no longer providing any extracontractual benefits, such as housing or medical care. The few Filipino women who came to Hawaii received substantially less—about 70 cents a day in 1915. Most workers were

Filipinos provided labor in Hawaii's sugar refineries as well as in the fields.

paid by how much they cut or planted in a single day rather than by the hour, which encouraged them to work hard and fast.

The workers lived on the plantations in facilities provided for them by the owners. The majority of workers, who were without their families, lived one or two to a room in large buildings that resembled barracks or dormitories; families had small four-room houses to themselves. A typical plantation usually featured some sort of recreation building where dances and other social activities could be held. Sports played an important part in plantation social life. Filipinos enjoyed baseball, volleyball, boxing, and pool. Both on and off the plantation, Filipinos tended to socialize most often with members of their own language group—Visayans with Visayans, Tagalogs with Tagalogs, and Ilocanos with Ilocanos.

Because life in the barrios was traditionally centered around the family, the absence of wives or prospective marriage partners was particularly difficult for Filipino immigrants to bear. To compensate, men from the same barrio or region would often establish a sort of communal household and surrogate family known as the *compang*. Members of a compang shared living quarters and chores; the oldest member acted as head of the household.

Joining Together

By 1929, almost 70 percent of the male workers on Hawaii's 41 major sugar plantations were Filipinos. The growers appreciated not only their capacity for hard labor but their willingness to work cheap. Initially grateful just for the opportunity to work, all too aware that they could be replaced by another, Filipinos were reluctant to demand improvements in their working conditions. Many felt it was simply not worth the effort to attempt to change a system that they only intended to be a part of for a few years. There was almost no tradition of organized labor in the Philippines, and the plantation system served to keep Filipinos isolated from other workers with whom they might join together. The language and cultural differences among Filipino immigrants—differences that the plantation owners intentionally fostered in making housing arrangements and work assignments—also helped keep them from uniting.

By the mid-1920s, however, the sheer number of Filipino workers on the plantations and mills gave them a certain amount of power to demand change. During that decade Filipino plantation workers united with Japanese workers to form their first labor unions. Their initial efforts were not very successful; strikes for better pay and conditions led to riots and retaliation by planters and civil authorities long accustomed to a compliant labor force. In 1924, a riot related to a strike on the island of Kauai resulted in the death of 16 Filipino workers and 4 policemen. This changed in the 1930s with the introduction of New Deal legislation that guaranteed workers the right to form unions and have those unions engage in collective bargaining on their behalf. The efforts of Filipino agricultural workers to organize finally paid off in 1940, when workers signed their first union contract with a Hawaiian sugar grower, the McBryde Sugar Company. By 1946 almost all Filipino plantation and sugar refinery workers had become members of the International Longshoremen's and Warehousemen's Union, which secured them such benefits as tenure and pension plans. By 1950 Hawaiian agricultural workers were the highest paid in the world.

Life on the Mainland

Hawaii may have been the primary destination for Filipinos seeking to work in the United States, but for many it became merely the first stop on the way to the U.S. mainland. From 1907 to 1929 almost 700 Filipino workers per year left Hawaii for California and other states. By 1929, it was estimated that one-fourth of the Filipinos on the mainland had come from Hawaii. Most of the Filipino immigrants to the continental United States tended to stay in California because of the availability of the same sort of agricultural work they had done at home and in Hawaii, because of the presence of established Filipino communities there, and because it was expensive to travel farther east within the United States. Those Filipinos who had come to California and other states from Hawaii were joined by thousands of other newcomers who emigrated directly from the Philippines. By 1930 some 50,000 Filipinos lived in the United States. As was the case with Filipino immigrants to Hawaii, the great majority were young, single men.

Filipinos found life on the mainland much different from what they had known in Hawaii or in their homeland. Few came to the United States with a signed contract that guaranteed them a job, as was the case with immigrants to Hawaii. There was plenty of work in the fruit and vegetable fields, but the growing season in California was much shorter than it was in Hawaii, and the growers did not provide such benefits as year-round housing. During the spring and summer many Filipinos worked in the fields planting and picking asparagus, lettuce, strawberries, sugar beets, and potatoes; during the winter months they worked in the city as waiters, domestic servants, or in other positions that were usually too low paying to appeal to Ameri-

Some of the Filipino laborers in this photograph taken in California's Salinas Valley in 1930 were 15 years old or younger. Magnos Cabreros, who was a young Pinoy farmhand in California in the 1920s, recalled working from sunup to sundown and crying in his bed at night from sheer exhaustion.

Alaskeros *was the Pinoy term for those Filipino immigrants who went north to Alaska to find jobs in the salmon canneries there. During the late 1930s as many as 9,000 Filipino Americans worked in Alaska.*

can men. A small number of Filipinos went north, to Alaska, where they took jobs cleaning and preparing salmon for processing in canneries. Because of the seasonal nature of the work available, the typical Filipino worker on the mainland drifted from job to job, living in different towns, cities, and even states throughout the year, wherever work was available at the highest wages.

Despite the hardships of life for Asian immigrants, the number of young Filipino men who came to the United States during the 1920s rose. A 1930 survey of Filipinos in the United States (excluding Hawaii) estimated that 20,000 Filipinos were employed as agricultural workers; 11,000 as domestic servants; and 4,200 in the Alaskan salmon industry. Many of the immigrants had been inspired to come by the success of others from their towns and villages who had gone to America and come back rich, or at least better educated. These Pinoys knew of the relatively large sums of money their countrymen had sent back to the Philippines, money that enabled the recipients to eat better, wear nicer clothes, and purchase their own land and homes. Desire to go to America was also reinforced by what Filipinos had learned of the United States in the schools that had been established for them by the Americans. American schoolbooks portraying the American way of life depicted a higher standard of living than was available to most Filipinos. These books and lessons increased the Filipinos' desire to make more money and live better. Finally, Filipinos were taught that America was a land of both economic and social opportunity, where jobs were available and the ideals of equality and justice for all were held in the highest regard.

For many immigrants, jobs were easier to find than fair treatment. Filipinos were shocked by the virulence of the discrimination and prejudice they were made to suffer by white Americans. In his book *Sound of Falling Light: Letters in Exile*, Carlos Bulosan, a Filipino-American writer, describes the confusion and hurt Filipino immigrants felt upon discovering that not all Americans were able to practice the high-minded sentiments

(continued on page 57)

REBIRTH AND REMEMBRANCE

Overleaf: *Eager to begin their life in the United States, Filipino immigrants attend a seminar for new arrivals at the Philippine Consulate in New York City. Since 1965, more immigrants have come to the United States from the Philippines than from any other country except Mexico.*

Thousands of Filipinos have immigrated to the United States during the 20th century, seeking better employment opportunities and an escape from the poverty and political corruption in their native land. The repression that occurred during the regime of dictatorial president Ferdinand Marcos is bitterly remembered by Filipino Americans today in the form of skits satirizing the deposed president and his wife, Imelda (top left), in protest demonstrations at the United Nations Building in New York City (lower right) and in performances that celebrate the presidency of Corazon Aquino (top right).

The Folklorico Filipino dance company performs a traditional Muslim dance from the Mindanao region of the Philippines at Lincoln Center in New York City for the Asian/Pacific American Heritage Festival (top), while a Filipino theatrical troupe stages a drama highlighting important events in Philippine history (left). Filipino organizations in the United States work hard to preserve their native culture and keep their heritage alive.

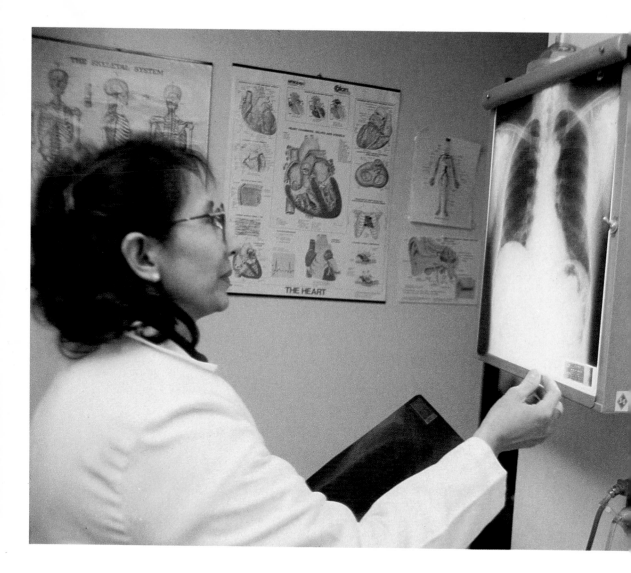

Filipinos have made significant contributions to many professions in the United States. In the past two decades the Philippines has supplied the United States with many physicians, such as Esperanza Angeles, seen examining an X ray above. Some Filipinos in the New York City area own or work in restaurants specializing in their native cuisine (top right) or manage and maintain buildings, as does Tony Quintos (right).

The task of building a new life in the
United States is never easy for new
immigrants. Rodolfo Sakdalan was unable
to find work in the United States as a
photojournalist, his profession in the
Philippines, so he currently makes his
living as a doorman in New York City.
Although the rampant corruption and lack
of economic opportunity in the Philippines
have left Sakdalan resigned to remaining in
the United States, memories of the homeland
remain strong. "When I dream," he says,
"it is always of the Philippines."

(continued from page 48)
expressed in the Declaration of Independence, the Pledge of Allegiance, and elsewhere:

> Western people are brought up to regard Orientals or colored peoples as inferior, but the mockery of it all is that Filipinos are taught to regard Americans as our equals. Adhering to our American ideals, living American life, these are contributory to our feeling of equality. The terrible truth in America shatters the Filipinos' dream of fraternity.

Anti-Filipino discrimination showed itself in many ways—uneasy glances and mistrustful whispers on the street and in stores were some of the subtler manifestations. More obviously, Filipinos were denied service in restaurants and barbershops and were barred from public pools, movie theaters, tennis courts, and other recreational facilities. Discrimination also affected the Filipinos in their quest for housing and jobs. Denied access to the finer neighborhoods of cities such as San Francisco and Los Angeles because of poverty and discrimination, Filipinos were forced to seek housing in the poorer neighborhoods of the inner city. They naturally sought out areas where other countrymen lived; the Filipino neighborhoods that developed were often called Little Manilas, after the homeland's capital. Poverty brought with it related social problems—crime, alcohol abuse, and prostitution.

Discrimination and poverty were related problems. Filipinos were discriminated against both because of the color of their skin and because they were poor; they were poor, at least in part, because they were discriminated against. The jobs available to Filipinos generally paid much lower wages than those available to white American laborers. Unskilled and illiterate white European immigrants were often able to find employment in factories, mills, mines, and other heavy industry, but for the most part these options did not exist for Filipinos. Factories were often unionized, and the unions did not allow Filipinos to join. Filipinos who were fortunate enough to obtain factory positions often were paid a lower wage than their

Stockton, California, was home to a large community of Filipino Americans in the 1930s, but they were rarely made to feel welcome. Many Filipinos were shocked by the discrepancy between the United States's promise of liberty and justice for all and its treatment of minorities, particularly Asians.

white counterparts, and their presence was resented by the other workers, who feared that the factory owners would begin to expect everyone to work at the lower wage. Even those Filipinos who learned job skills or professions in school were often not given a chance to practice them. Engineers and other technicians could not get jobs that allowed them to use their skills, and, depending on the state, Filipinos who received a law or medical degree from an American school often were not allowed to practice. Anti-Asian prejudice was even codified as law; until 1946 Filipinos and other Asians could not become citizens.

So most Filipino immigrants to the mainland in the early part of the 20th century were forced to work in agriculture. By 1930, 82 percent of all Filipinos in the United States were employed as farm laborers; 5 percent lived and worked in California. These farm workers planted celery; hoed rows of sugar beets; picked peaches, grapes, melons, tomatoes, apricots, pears and cherries; harvested rice and lettuce; and cut, washed, and sorted asparagus. Often, Filipinos served as the foremen for these work crews, and some even became *padrones*, contractors who arranged with a farm owner to provide the labor to harvest or sow his crops. The grower paid the padrone an agreed-upon sum; the padrone then paid the workers. Obviously, it was in the padrone's interest to keep wages as low as possible in order to increase his own profits. The padrone also supplied his men with food and sometimes shelter. The cost of these necessities was deducted from the workers' salaries. As in Hawaii, the harvesters were paid by how much they picked rather than by an hourly or daily wage. Like their Hawaiian counterparts, Filipino agricultural workers in California and other states tried to organize themselves and fight for higher wages, but these efforts did not receive the recognition of farm workers until the 1960s, when the Agricultural Workers Organizing Committee, led by Filipino-American Larry Dulay Itliong, merged with the National Farm Workers Organization, led by Cesar Chavez. The new organization, called the United Farm Workers Organizing Committee, was successful in obtaining better wages and working conditions for the farm laborers, although many injustices still exist.

The Dark Side of the American Dream

Despite housing and job discrimination, Filipino Americans did not feel the full brunt of anti-Asian discrimination until the late 1920s. Whereas employers continued to value Filipinos as hardworking (and poorly paid) employees, other Americans viewed them and other Asian immigrants as a "yellow peril" that threatened to overrun the United States and destroy the American way of life. Beginning in 1928, Filipinos became the target of violent attacks. That year also saw the beginning of political movements calling for an end to further Filipino immigration and legislation to deport those already in the country. The increased prevalence and vehemence of such racist sentiment was in some part due to the increased number of Filipino immigrants in the United States—60,000 by 1930. Americans had long worried that their country would be overrun by foreigners, who would infest the United States with alien values and customs, a viewpoint expressed by Senator Albert Johnson of Washington, the primary architect of the Immigration Act of 1924. Johnson said that Americans were tired of

The famed photographer Dorothea Lange captured this image of Filipino-American lettuce pickers in California's Imperial Valley during the waning days of the Great Depression.

the encroachments of the foreign-born flood upon their own lives. They have come to realize that such a flood, affecting as it does every individual of whatever race or origin, cannot fail likewise

to affect the institutions which have made and preserved American liberties. It is no wonder, therefore, that the myth of the melting pot has been discredited. It is no wonder that Americans everywhere are insisting that their land no longer shall offer free and unrestricted asylum to the rest of the world.

The United States is our land. If it was not the land of our fathers, at least it may be, and it should be, the land of our children. We intend to maintain it so. The day of unalloyed welcome to all peoples, the day of indiscriminate acceptance of all races, has definitely ended.

As the number of Filipino immigrants grew, Americans worried that they would take jobs away from American citizens, a fear that increased after the 1929 collapse of the stock market and the economic devastation wreaked by the depression. Americans were also disturbed because so many of the Filipino immigrants were men. Filipino males outnumbered women 14 to 1. Most were young; few had a wife back home. Quite naturally, these young men often sought female companionship, but their opportunities for socializing with members of the opposite sex were limited.

The opportunities for marriage between Filipinos and white women were limited both by prejudice and law. By the time Filipinos began to arrive in California in large numbers, the state had already enacted anti-miscegenation laws, which prohibited whites from marrying blacks, Mongolians (an imprecise term intended to apply to all Asians), or mulattoes. In 1933, a Filipino man, Salvador Roldan, challenged the law after he and his white fiancée were refused a marriage license in Los Angeles. He claimed the laws only prohibited marriage between whites and Mongolians, not between whites and Malays. Roldan won his case, but the state was quick to pass a law that included Malays in the prohibition. Mixed couples who wished to marry had to go to Utah or other nearby states.

Public opinion regulated other attempts by Filipino men to socialize with white women. Contact between Filipino men and white women often occurred at

Cannery workers, some of them Filipinos, on strike in Seattle, Washington, in April 1939. For the most part Filipino-American workers were poorly paid and ill treated.

dance halls where Filipinos and other patrons paid to dance with young women employed by the hall's owners. These dancers for hire were called taxi dancers. The sight of Filipino men and white women socializing together enraged many white Americans, who concluded that Filipinos were "a bad social influence."

As feelings began to mount against the Filipinos, politicians and private citizens began to move against them at the same time, the former by proposing anti-Filipino legislation, the latter through vigilante action. Efforts were made at the local, state, and national levels of government to deal with "the Filipino problem." In 1928, a California congressman proposed a bill in the U.S. House of Representatives that would effectively ban all Filipinos from the United States by giving them immigrant status—Filipinos were then U.S. nationals, not immigrants—thus making them subject to the strict Immigration Act of 1924. The law did not pass, but other attempts to limit Filipino immigration followed. In 1929 the California state legislature passed a resolution asking that no more Filipinos be allowed to enter the country. Private organizations passed similar resolutions; these included local and state federations of labor, the national and powerful American Federation of Labor, and the American Legion and other "patriotic" groups.

At the same time, violent confrontations between whites and Filipinos were on the rise. The first anti-Filipino "riots" were not much more than scuffles that took place between whites and Filipinos in agricultural regions of California and Washington. Although these fistfights were not very serious—few people were injured—they were widely reported in newspapers all over the West Coast, helping to convince a public already predisposed to believe that Filipinos were lascivious, alcoholic lawbreakers that radical solutions to the immigrant problem were needed. Few readers cared that the taunts and attacks of young white men were often responsible for the outbreaks of violence.

The continuing tension between whites and Filipinos made it inevitable that other, more serious outbreaks would occur. In Exeter, a small farming town in California's fertile San Joaquin Valley, months of verbal and physical assaults on the Filipinos who worked the grape and fig orchards there culminated in a full-blown riot in October 1929. Different accounts of the riot's origins exist—some say whites began rioting when a Filipino showed up with a white girl at a local carnival; others say it started when Filipinos threw stones at an Italian truck driver who had been taunting them. On October 24, hundreds of local white farm workers banded together and visited every farm in the area where Filipinos were employed, demanding that they be dismissed and replaced with white

Filipino men dressed in their Sunday best relax at a migrant labor camp in California's San Joaquin Valley. On Sundays, Filipino agricultural workers enjoyed a brief respite from the week's labors.

workers and smashing and burning cars and farm facilities if the request was refused. A later inquiry into
the matter by the state's industrial commission found
that although the rioters complained that the Filipinos
were taking jobs away from native whites, few whites
took the positions created after the Filipinos had been
fired.

News of the Exeter riot traveled fast, and it had a
particularly deleterious effect on race relations in Watsonville, a small town in the hills of west-central California, near the coast. Watsonville grew one-fourth of
all the lettuce that was exported from California. Its
growers relied heavily on immigrant labor, but relations between Filipinos and the town's white citizens
had long been very poor. Racial tensions were aggravated by reports of the violence in Exeter and the passage of a resolution in January 1930 by the Chamber
of Commerce of nearby northern Monterey County
that condemned Filipinos as an undesirable social influence, particularly on young girls. The resolution de-
manded that all Filipinos be expelled from the county.
A local Filipino organization, the Northern Monterey
Filipino Club, responded by flooding the area with leaf-
lets denouncing the resolution and its author, a local
judge. No violence occurred until the opening of a taxi-
dance hall for Filipinos (with white women as dance
partners) in a beach town a few miles away. Locals
picketed the dance hall; on the night of January 19 the
situation turned ugly. Gangs of young white men
marched on the hall, attacked Filipinos there, and fired
shots into passing cars. The assaults continued over
the following days. A mob of 400 whites ransacked the
Northern Monterey Filipino Club, and a crowd of
young white residents raided the Filipino quarters at
a local farm and fired shots into a bunkhouse that
killed a young Filipino worker, Fermin Tovera. The
death finally persuaded the local citizens to act to end
the rioting.

Tovera's death provoked outrage in the Philippines. February 2—the day his body arrived back
there—was declared National Humiliation Day, in protest of the riots and the poor treatment Filipinos re-

ceived in the United States, and Tovera was proclaimed a national hero. Eight young Americans were finally convicted in Tovera's death, but they received extremely light sentences. Four were minors and were not required to serve time in jail; the other four were imprisoned for one month and then put on probation.

Closing the Door

American resentment of Filipino immigrants worked to benefit their homeland in its quest for independence. As news of Watsonville spread, more riots erupted up and down the coast. Filipinos were banned from some towns and villages. Late-night attacks on Filipino janitors and restaurant workers were reported in San Francisco. The Filipino Center in Stockton, California, was bombed. The growth in anti-Filipino sentiment led to renewed efforts to restrict Filipino immigration, but that could only be done by altering the Philippines's legal status. The U.S. Congress took steps to move the Philippines closer to independence, which accorded with the desires of the Filipinos themselves. Advocating immediate independence, the Nacionalista party had long dominated local and national elections in the Philippines, and Filipino leaders constantly petitioned U.S. government leaders for their nation's freedom. But their pleas met with little success until Americans, for reasons of their own, also asked their government to revise its policy concerning the Philippines. The resulting Tydings-McDuffie Independence Act in 1934 finally put an end to large-scale Filipino immigration. The Philippines became a U.S. commonwealth, and an immigration quota of 50 Filipinos per year was established.

Send Them Back

Those convinced that there were too many Filipinos did not wish to stop with the Tydings-McDuffie Act. That legislation essentially ended immigration, but it still left some 45,000 Filipinos in the United States. In 1935, the U.S. Congress passed the Repatriation Act,

which provided free transportation back to the Philippines for Filipinos who wished to return. Supporters of the legislation argued that its intent was humanitarian. As some of the poorest members of American society, Filipinos suffered greatly as a result of the Great Depression. Many lost their jobs, but because they were not citizens, Filipinos could not qualify for any of the relief programs established as part of Franklin Roosevelt's New Deal. The Repatriation Act was designed to help these suffering immigrants by allowing them to return to their homeland. Despite the hardship they endured here, few Filipinos availed themselves of the opportunity to leave. By 1937, only 7,400 Filipinos had returned home; the rate of repatriation slowed even more over the next few years as the economy improved.

Filipino-American field hands take a moment's rest on a California asparagus farm in the early 1930s. For paltry wages, Filipinos plowed the land, planted crops, tended them during the growing season, and harvested them when they were ripe. Rarely did they earn enough to buy plots of their own.

Soldiers of the First Filipino Infantry Regiment of the U.S. Army take the oath of citizenship in 1943. Filipinos who served in the U.S. armed forces during World War II were allowed to become citizens; other Filipino Americans had to wait until 1946 for this privilege.

THE SECOND WAVE OF FILIPINO IMMIGRATION

The second wave of Filipino immigration to the United States began after World War II. The Philippines received their independence in 1946, and Filipinos who came to the United States after that date were officially classified as aliens. Because the Philippines was now an independent nation, its immigration quota was raised from 50 to 100, the same as other Asian countries were allowed under the Immigration Act of 1924. Although it did not become much easier for Filipinos to enter the United States, those here already benefited from changes in their legal status. Under legislation enacted in 1946, first-generation Filipino immigrants were able to become citizens under the same naturalization process as white European immigrants.

The postwar immigrants were quite different than the earlier generation. Rather than young men, the 100-a-year quotas were instead filled with the wives, children, and family members of the immigrants who had come before the war and settled here, as well as

Filipino sugar plantation workers in Hawaii in 1949. As a result of the growing strength of Filipino labor unions in the years following World War II, working conditions and wages on the plantations improved.

with marriageable young Filipino women. Most settled in already established Filipino communities, the great majority of them on the West Coast. Together with the Filipinos already living here, these new immigrants settled down. These Filipino-American couples had children, who were by rights U.S. citizens, and the number of Filipino Americans slowly grew, from 98,535 in 1940 to 122,707 in 1950 to 176,310 in 1960. The proportion of Filipino females to Filipino males grew as well. By 1963, there were less than two Filipino males to every Filipino female.

Although the number of married Filipinos and Filipino families increased, economic opportunity remained limited. Because trade unions in California still did not allow Filipinos to join, there were few industrial and construction jobs available to them. As previously, many Filipinos were forced to work in agriculture, as domestic servants, and as waiters, cooks, and busboys. Most still worked on farms and plantations. In California in 1950, 55 percent of Filipino workers were agricultural laborers; 10 years later that figure was still high, at 31 percent.

Reopening the Door

Conditions affecting Filipino immigration changed greatly in the 1960s. In 1965, the U.S. Congress passed the Hart-Celler Immigration Act, which has remained the basis of U.S. immigration policy through the late 1980s. The Hart-Celler Act effectively abolished the immigration quota system that was based on national origins and substituted instead a quota system based on the personal qualifications of the immigrant. Professional skills and family relations to U.S. citizens and resident aliens became the relevant factors in deciding whether to admit an immigration applicant. Filipinos took full advantage of the new law. The number of Filipino immigrants to the United States jumped to 6,093 in 1966 and increased fivefold, to 31,203, by 1970. Since 1965, more immigrants have come to the United States from the Philippines than from any other country except Mexico.

President Lyndon Johnson signs the Immigration Act of 1965 on New York's Liberty Island. With him are Vice-president Hubert Humphrey (front, third from left) and Attorney General Robert Kennedy (front, second from right).

A New Type of Immigrant

Post–World War II immigrants, such as Fabian Bergano, a Seattle pharmacist, tended to be better educated than their prewar counterparts.

The new Filipino immigrants were more likely to be educated professionals than unskilled agricultural laborers. The majority of them qualified for admission under the new immigration law as "professional, technical and kindred workers." They were teachers, doctors, nurses, engineers, accountants, dentists, pharmacists, and others with college degrees whom the United States welcomed because it needed people with their skills. In the 1970s, the Philippines led all other countries in providing the United States with new engineers, physicians, and technical workers. Most of them were able to obtain jobs immediately in their chosen professions, although others—including many dentists, doctors, and pharmacists—had to undergo more training in order to meet U.S. licensing requirements. These new immigrants settled not just in California and Hawaii but in urban centers across the United States, particularly New York and Chicago.

Another characteristic of post-1965 Filipino immigration that distinguished it from earlier waves was that the typical immigrant was no longer a young, single male. Because these new immigrants intended to stay in the United States, whole families tended to emigrate together. When that was not possible, one member would come to the United States alone in the hope of being able to earn enough money to eventually bring the rest of the family over.

Indeed, this intention of making a permanent home in the United States was perhaps the most profound difference between the new immigrants and their predecessors. The new generation did not dream of working for a few years in the United States, making a lot of money, and returning home in triumph as rich men and women. Instead, the Filipino immigrants who entered under the Hart-Celler Act were convinced that they would find long-term opportunities in the United States that were simply unavailable in the Philippines. For various reasons, they believed that the only way to fulfill their dreams was to say good-bye forever to their native land and move to America.

Why They Came

Independence had not solved all of the Philippines's problems. The poverty that had plagued the country since the days of Spanish rule continued and proved difficult to eradicate. Land ownership remained concentrated in the hands of a privileged elite. Trade and budget deficits—each year the government spent more money than it collected in revenues, and the Philippines annually imported more goods than it exported—further aggravated the nation's economic woes.

The democratic system of government installed by the United States did not function as well as its supporters had hoped. Corruption existed at every level of government, from the local all the way up to the national. People received government jobs not because they were qualified for them but because they knew or were related to someone important. Government leaders did everything they could to promote their own family businesses. Democracy was supposed to ensure that all Filipinos had a say in how their nation

Filipinos harvest rice on the island of Luzon. Widespread economic progress did not accompany the Philippines's achievement of political independence, a failure that continued to spur immigration to the United States.

Poverty and overpopulation are two of the problems that have troubled the Philippines since World War II.

was governed, through the exercise of the right to vote, but the system did not always function as it was intended to. Election fraud, extortion, voter intimidation, the buying and selling of votes, and political murder were not uncommon. The elections in 1947, the first year of independence, were marked by bloodshed and widespread fraud. The 1949 presidential election was even worse. It was estimated that more than one-fifth of the registered votes cast were done so illegally. As a *Reader's Digest* writer commented, "Every device known to fraudulent elections was used. . . . Filipinos sadly wisecracked that even the birds and the bees voted in some precincts." Neither Manuel Roxas y Acuña, Elpidio Quirino, Ramón Magsaysay, Carlos García, or Diosdado Macapagal, the Philippines's first five elected presidents, was able to put an end to poverty or corruption. The extremely popular Magsaysay enjoyed the most success in addressing his nation's problems, but his term of office was cut short when he was killed in a plane crash in March 1957.

All of these problems grew worse during the presidency of Ferdinand Marcos, who was first elected to the office in 1965. Both Marcos and his wife, Imelda, came from prestigious but not particularly wealthy families. Marcos began his political career in 1949, when he was elected to the Filipino congress. Like other Filipino politicians before him, Marcos profited personally from his power and connections, using his office to enhance his wealth in a practice that Filipinos called "crony capitalism." What set Marcos apart was the sheer magnitude of his greed. During his first term as president, Marcos made millions of dollars by forcing businesses to cut him in on a share of their profits. Should they refuse to do so, they might be targeted for government investigation, have their tax and financial records audited, or find themselves the target of special government legislation.

Marcos was reelected in 1969, following a campaign that set new records for the Philippines in terms of money spent on campaigning, ballot fraud, assassinations, and voter intimidation. Determined to hang

The rampant corruption and repression that occurred during the presidency of Ferdinand Marcos ultimately turned virtually all segments of Philippine society against him.

An aging but confident President Ferdinand Marcos at the outset of the 1986 campaign in which he was opposed by Corazon Aquino. Marcos seriously misjudged the extent of the opposition to his regime.

on to his profitable position, Marcos bought enough votes in the Filipino congress to secure passage of a constitutional amendment that would allow him to run for a third term in office. (Like the U.S. Constitution, the Filipino constitution at that time only allowed the president to serve two terms.)

By this time, opposition to Marcos was widespread. While Marcos and his cronies diverted funds that could have been used for economic development into their own pockets, the already weak economy was further damaged by frequent strikes carried out by Filipino workers seeking a decent living. Millions of dollars in U.S. economic aid found its way to Marcos's private bank accounts. Communist guerrillas known as the New People's Army sought to foment revolution in the countryside among the peasantry, who for centuries had tilled the soil on property owned by other men. Demonstrations against Marcos's regime took place frequently. Concerned with the "instability" of the situation in the Philippines, American investors threatened to withdraw their funds.

After creating a climate of crisis by staging a series of attacks on members of his government, Marcos declared martial law on September 23, 1972, and awarded himself dictatorial powers. Freedom of the press and speech, free elections, and other democratic aspects of life in the Philippines came to an end. Political opponents were thrown in jail. Hundreds of businesses—sugar refineries, pineapple plantations, coconut farms and processing plants, public utilities, railroads, taxicab companies, radio and television stations, newspapers, airlines—were nationalized, which in this case meant seized by Marcos. Although Marcos had long promised land reform, his actions seemed to indicate that what he meant was redistributing all property among himself, his family, and his friends. Under the direction of Marcos and his rapacious cronies, the Filipino economy reeled. The already poor standard of living plummeted. By the mid-1970s, 40 percent of all deaths in the Philippines were attributable to malnutrition.

The excesses of the Marcos regime opened the floodgates of emigration. In the period following his

Benigno "Ninoy" Aquino discusses his planned return to the Philippines at a press conference held in San Francisco, California, on July 26, 1983. Less than one month later he would be dead, and Filipinos feared that their hopes for democratic reform in their country had expired with him.

declaration of martial law, the number of Filipinos who emigrated to the United States never totaled less than 30,000 in a single year. Unfortunately for the Philippines, these thousands of emigrants for the most part represented the elite of Filipino society, as only the most educated applicants were granted visas to the United States. Poor and uneducated Filipinos had just as strong a desire to take advantage of the greater oportunities available in the United States but under the terms of the Hart-Celler act were unable to gain admission. Although the new immigrants made immediate contributions to American society, this "brain drain" simply aggravated the problems of the Philippines by depriving that nation of the abilities of its educated professionals. Yet two of the Filipinos who left their country for the United States at that time— Senator Benigno Aquino, Jr., a prominent politician and Marcos's chief political rival, and his wife, Corazon—were to prove instrumental in shaping the destiny of their homeland.

The Laigo family of Seattle,
Washington, photographed in
1945. Kinship and family
are extremely important to
Filipino Americans.

GOD AND FAMILY

Although several generations of Filipinos have now immigrated to the United States and many have adopted American lifestyles, there are many cultural values and traditions that still give Filipino Americans a distinct identity among others in the American melting pot. Among the values cherished by Filipinos in their ancestral land and in the United States is a belief in the importance of family, education, and religion.

Traditionally for Filipinos, the family, rather than the self, is the center of existence. A young person's decisions regarding his or her future—what career to choose, whom to marry—are often made on the basis of what is best for the family rather than on what is best for that person as an individual.

Filipinos typically live with three generations—grandparents, parents, and children—under one roof. But the concept of family extends well beyond this relatively small group to include all relatives of both the father and mother. Family businesses are quite common. Children are taught to have enormous respect for their elders among this extended family. Filipino Christians also emphasize the importance of godparents, friends or relatives chosen at the time of an infant's baptism who agree to take responsibility for the child's religious education. Godparents also sometimes help support the child financially and in general look out for the child's welfare. Godparents who are not blood relatives become honorary kinsmen.

In one sense, this otherwise honorable allegiance to family has helped contribute to the enormous amount of corruption in Philippine politics and business. In their ancestral country, because of the many hardships life entailed, many Filipinos developed an attitude known there as Lamangan, which roughly translated means "by hook or by crook to get on top." When one can rely only on one's family, then one gives primary allegiance to the family rather than the nation or abstract ideals of fairness or justice. One is therefore likely to choose family members over those who could be considered more qualified for political appointments or jobs.

Yet because this belief in family loyalty emphasizes helping others as well as oneself, it has been of inestimable value in helping Filipino immigrants and their children make their way in their adopted homeland. Filipino Americans are their own best allies in the United States, encouraging and helping each other achieve the best that this country can provide—for example, by bringing relatives over here as new immigrants, helping them find jobs and housing, or even by simply sending money back to the Philippines to ease the poverty of those still living there.

Strong Women

One distinguishing aspect of Philippine culture is the leading role played by women in both the family and in the society at large. In Philippine culture, women have been considered the equal of men for thousands of years. The influence of the male-dominated Spanish culture did little to change this. Even in the early 20th century, the Filipino women were often better educated than the men. Within the family, it is the woman who decides how much money is spent and on what. And in Philippine society, women hold public office and executive and professional positions at all levels.

A Reverence for Learning

Filipino Americans of both sexes consider education to be extremely important. The history of Filipino immigration to the United States began with students de-

Many young Filipinos came to the United States in order to obtain a college education, intending to return to the Philippines to put their knowledge to use to benefit their homeland. Belen de Guzman Braganza (left) and a friend, students at the University of Washington, posed for this photograph in 1934.

termined to avail themselves of the varied educational opportunities not open to them at home, and the current generation of Filipino Americans values education no less keenly. American colleges and universities are filled with Filipino immigrants pursuing professional and other advanced degrees, in the belief that learning—and professional certification—is the key to advancement in American society. The vast majority of Filipino-American students finish their high school educations. In 1980, the U.S. Census found that 74.2 percent of all Filipinos 25 or older had graduated from high school, and 37 percent had 4 or more years of college.

The great majority of Filipinos are Roman Catholics; they carried their faith with them to the United States. Here, Filipino sugar plantation workers pose outside the church they built at Eiva, Hawaii, on the fifth anniversary of its establishment, September 1920.

Religious Beliefs

Religion, particularly the Catholic faith, plays an integral part in the life of many Filipino Americans. The vast majority of the population of the Philippines is

Filipino Americans celebrate José Rizal Day—December 30—in Honolulu, Hawaii, in 1918.

Roman Catholic, and similar statistics apply to Filipino Americans. Although many Filipino men are religious, it is traditionally the women who are most active in practicing the faith, which is perhaps the major reason why Filipino-American churches were not established in the United States until well after World War II, when Filipino women began immigrating in large number.

Church rituals mark the most important milestones of a Filipino's life—baptism, confirmation, marriage, and death—and the most joyous Philippine holidays are connected with the church. In the barrios of the homeland, these celebrations helped the people temporarily forget the hardships of their daily life. Yet in America, where life is presumably better, these traditions are still carried on, particularly in cities such as Los Angeles and San Francisco and in Hawaii, where large communities of Filipino Americans live. Weddings, confirmations, anniversaries, and baptisms are the occasion for jubilant parties, traditionally celebrated with huge quantities of food prepared by Filipino hostesses eager to outdo one another. On these festive days, friends and strangers alike are welcomed into the homes of the celebrants. But no holidays are celebrated with as much joy and ceremony as the most important holy days—Holy Week, Easter Sunday, and especially the time around Christmas.

The Christmas Season

Filipino Catholics traditionally celebrate Christmas for more than a week leading up to the holy day itself. Beginning on December 16, masses are celebrated early every morning, up until Christmas Day, December 25. Throughout the festival period, children and adults stroll from home to home singing Christmas carols, often accompanied by a string band or a guitarist. The highlight of the whole celebratory period is the midnight Christmas Eve mass, known as the Misa de Gallo, and the various events that precede it.

Prior to the Misa de Gallo, there is a competition among communities to see who has built the largest *parol*, or lantern, especially for the occasion. Like the Christmas tree for most Americans, the parol serves Filipinos as a symbol of the Christmas holiday. The Christmas Eve celebration continues with Panunulayan, a traditional procession through the streets of the town or village. A woman and a man—or a girl and a boy—dressed as Mary, the mother of Jesus, and her husband, Joseph, lead the procession. They reenact the story of Christ's birth as they stop nine times to request shelter so that Mary can have her baby and

Music was one way Filipino Americans relaxed when they were not working. Many immigrants delighted in playing the songs they had known in the old country, but these workers on a Hawaii plantation formed a band to perform a distinctly American music— jazz.

81

are nine times turned away. The procession ends at the church with the mass and the celebration of the birth.

The rites surrounding the birth of Christ continue in January during a 10-day period known as the fiesta season. This holiday period is intended to focus the community's attention on the values of charity and understanding that Jesus Christ is said to have imparted to his disciples. Beginning on January 6, daily masses are held to honor the Christ child. The holiday ends 10 days later with the Feast of El Niño—the holy infant—climaxing with a procession in which an image of the Christ child is brought to the church.

These religious observances and related dramas, such as the Panunulayan, were introduced to the Philippines by the Spanish as a way to make Christianity more appealing to the Filipinos, who already enacted many similar dramas associated with non-Christian rituals. Others include the Sinakulo, which is performed throughout the week from Palm Sunday to Easter Sunday and dramatizes the life, crucifixion, and resurrection of Christ, and the Salubong, which depicts the meeting of Christ and his mother on Easter Sunday following his resurrection.

Like other immigrant groups, Filipinos must balance the need to assimilate with the desire to preserve familiar culture and values. These Filipino-American musicians in New York City are giving a recital on traditional instruments.

Beauty pageant winners fill the rostrum at a Hilo, Hawaii, gathering of the Filipino Federation of America.

Secular Celebrations

Secular holidays are celebrated by the Filipino communities in the United States with traditional Filipino music and dance. The *rondalla*, or string band, provides some of the favorite Filipino music. A typical rondalla is composed of folk string instruments ranging from the one-string *bajo de unas* to the 14-string *banduria*.

Filipinos are also fond of performing their many traditional folk dances, some of which require special skills. Couples dance the *fandango saw ila* while balancing an oil lamp on top of the head and in each hand. Practitioners of the *tinikling* dance over and around long bamboo poles, which are held close to the ground and clapped together in rhythms different from those the dancers move to. Many Filipino organizations in America are dedicated to seeing that these traditional expressions of culture are not lost.

Another enduring custom is the beauty pageant; one is usually held during every festival. Filipino customs also include such perhaps less respectable pursuits as cockfights, in which prize roosters fight to the death, and gambling, which is often connected with cockfights. Cockfighting, known to Filipinos as *sabong*, has been illegal in the United States for many decades, but that has not stopped Filipinos—particularly the older generation—from pursuing one of their favorite pastimes.

SUCCESS IN A NEW WORLD

Although they have been coming to the United States in large numbers for only a short time in comparison with many other immigrant groups—indeed, the greatest number of Filipino immigrants have arrived only since the mid-1960s—Filipino Americans have distinguished themselves, both in this country and internationally, as achievers in a number of different fields. Because of the unique historical relationship between the United States and the Philippines, other Filipinos have called this country home for a short while and then returned to the Philippines, where they have made contributions in a number of different areas. Perhaps the most famous of these returned Filipino immigrants is Corazon Aquino, who succeeded Ferdinand Marcos as president of the Philippines in 1986, and her late husband, Benigno.

Arts and Sports

In art, Orlando S. Lagman, who once served as a U.S. seaman, became one of the leading portrait painters of his day. Lagman was chosen to paint the official portraits of U.S. presidents Dwight D. Eisenhower, John F. Kennedy, Lyndon B. Johnson, and Richard M.

During his years in the National Football League, Roman Gabriel's powerful arm made him a feared passer, while his size and strength made him perhaps the most difficult quarterback in the circuit to tackle.

Nixon. In music, Dalisay Aldaba, a Filipino-American woman, was selected in 1948 to play the leading role in the New York City Opera's production of *Madame Butterfly*.

Filipinos distinguished themselves in many sports, but they were most successful in boxing, particularly among the lighter-weight classes. During the 1930s and 1940s, four Filipino pugilists became world champions, but none were so well known as Francisco "Pancho Villa" Guilledo. Weighing in at 110 pounds and standing only 5 feet 1 inches tall, Guilledo became the flyweight champion of the world on June 18, 1923, when he dropped the legendary British fighter Jimmy Wilde during the seventh round of their championship bout before a packed house in New York City. Sadly, Guilledo's career was not to last long. Two years later, at the age of 24, he died of blood poisoning from an infected tooth. The winner of 103 of his 108 bouts, Guilledo was elected to the Boxing Hall of Fame in 1961.

The many other Filipino-American sports achievers include Vicki Manalo Draves, who in 1948 became the first woman in Olympic history to win a gold medal in the platform and springboard diving events, and Roman Gabriel, who was an all-American quarterback for North Carolina State University and then starred as a professional for 11 years with the Los Angeles Rams and the Philadelphia Eagles. In 1969, Gabriel was named the National Football League's Most Valuable Player and Player of the Year. Rawboned Jim Washington, a 6-foot 7-inch graduate of Villanova University, played for 10 years in the National Basketball Association, where his rebounding and smooth moves around the basket made him a valuable contributor to 5 different teams.

Telling Their Story

Many Filipino Americans have taken up the pen and become respected writers. Journalist Evaristo C. Pecson was honored in 1947 by the Eugene Field Society of the National Association of Authors and Journalists of America for his book *Our World: The Creation of the Universe from Early Times to the Present Day*. Written in

1944, at the height of World War II, the book is a reflection on the possibility of peace and justice in a world seemingly gone mad with war and other evils. Two other Filipino-American writers, Manuel Buaken and Carlos Bulosan, have written famous autobiographical accounts of their experiences in America during the first wave of Filipino immigration.

Buaken's *I Have Lived with the American People*, published in 1948, records the experiences of a young man who first came to America in the 1920s on a theology scholarship from Princeton University but turned his back on the chance to obtain an American college degree, which would have enabled him to return to his homeland with considerable prestige, and instead cast his lot with the Filipino community in America. Buaken worked for years as a restaurant chef, houseboy, and farm worker before finally earning his degree. He also details the mistreatment that Filipino Americans endured as a result of racial prejudice as well as the opportunities that his experience in America offered him.

Bulosan's *America Is in the Heart: A Personal History*, which was published in 1946, became a classic of the Asian-American ethnic awareness revival of the 1970s. Bulosan came to America in 1930 to work with other Filipinos in the fields, but with his frail physique and sickly constitution, he could not withstand the strenuous labor. Instead, he immersed himself in the literature of the world in the libraries of California and emerged as a writer, poet, and radical labor organizer by the early 1940s. *America Is in the Heart* tells the story of his life, from his birth in the Philippines as the son of Ilocano peasants to his writing successes, but it is also the story of the struggles of the Filipino community in the United States to overcome racism and poverty during the years of the Great Depression.

Law and Labor

Fittingly enough, considering the many legal obstacles that were erected to keep them from enjoying the full benefits of life in the United States, Filipino Americans have distinguished themselves in the field of law. A number of them have been rewarded by being ap-

Carlos Bulosan, the son of Ilocano peasants, achieved success in the United States as a writer. He also devoted much of his time and energy to activities in support of the labor movement.

Pablo Manlapit (right) organized Hawaii's first Filipino labor union, the Filipino Federation of Labor, in 1911.

pointed to judgeships or elected as political representatives. In 1970, a California woman, Marion Lacadia Obera, was named as the first Filipino-American judge in the continental United States by then governor Ronald Reagan. In Hawaii, where in 1980 Filipino Americans constituted 14 percent of the population, they have been especially successful. Benjamin Menor, who immigrated to Hawaii in 1934 at the age of seven to join his father, an agricultural worker, achieved a number of firsts as a Filipino American. In 1962, he was elected to Hawaii's state senate, which made him the first Filipino American to serve in any state's legislature. Twelve years later Hawaii's governor appointed him to the state's supreme court, Hawaii's highest judicial body. He was the first Filipino American to serve on a supreme court in any state.

Many of the earliest Filipino Americans distinguished themselves as leaders of their people in the labor movement. These men organized agricultural laborers into unions for the purpose of working together to obtain higher wages and better working conditions. One of the most prominent was Pablo Manlapit. As a young man, he worked in the Philippines for many years on government projects until he was dismissed for attempting to organize fellow employees into labor unions. Manlapit then signed up to be an agricultural worker in the United States and boarded a ship for Hawaii. He distinguished himself as a smart and hard worker on the plantations and was promoted to supervisory jobs, but he was not content with personal success. After witnessing firsthand how hard his fellow Filipinos worked in the sugarcane and pineapple fields and how little control they had over their own wages and working conditions, Manlapit soon turned his energies once again to labor organizing.

In 1911, Manlapit founded Hawaii's first Filipino labor union, the Filipino Federation of Labor. He was soon fired from his plantation job for staging a strike for higher wages and went instead to work in a law office. In 1919, Manlapit became the first Filipino in Hawaii to be licensed as a lawyer, but while he was carrying on his legal studies, he was also devoting much time to union activities.

Under Manlapit's direction, the Filipino Federation of Labor began to cooperate with its Japanese counterpart. On January 19, 1920, the two unions launched the largest labor action ever seen in the Hawaiian islands. About 3,000 Filipino workers and hundreds more Japanese struck 4 sugar plantations. The strike lasted 165 days, yet plantation owners remained resistant to the workers' demands and no real progress was made. Beginning in April 1924, Manlapit helped stage another strike, with 3,000 workers striking 23 of Hawaii's 45 sugar plantations. This action turned violent: Hawaiian police attacked the union headquarters, and in the fight 16 Filipinos and 4 police officers were killed.

Manlapit was arrested as a result of the strike. After a trial that many people called blatantly unfair—it was alleged, for example, that prosecution witnesses against him were paid off—he was sentenced to 2 to 10 years' hard labor. Eventually he was deported to the Philippines, where he finished his career as a labor adviser to the Philippine government and to the U.S. Navy. But the union he started lived on. Two of his followers revived it in 1937, and after an 85-day strike in 1937, the Filipino Federation of Labor finally won the plantation workers a 15 percent pay hike. This early unionization of the Hawaiian workers led to the good working conditions and high pay they would enjoy compared to other agricultural laborers in the United States.

Although fewer of the post–World War II immigrants worked in agriculture, Filipinos were still strongly represented among California's fruit and vegetable pickers in the 1950s and 1960s and played a major part in the labor movements of those decades, particularly in what was perhaps the best-known agricultural strike of this century: the Great Grape Strike of 1965. The leader of Filipino-American farm workers at that time—and one of the founders of today's powerful agricultural workers union, the United Farm Workers Union (UFW)—was Larry Dulay Itliong.

Itliong was a farm worker in California in the 1950s, a time when organizations of agricultural laborers were still not recognized by California growers as legitimate

The members of the Filipino Labor Commission for Hawaii posed for this photograph after their meeting on November 17, 1923. The willingness of Filipino Americans to act collectively in order to obtain better working conditions resulted in Hawaiian agricultural workers becoming the highest paid such workers in the world by the 1950s.

unions with the right to bargain collectively on behalf of their members. The Filipino Farm Labor Union (FFLU), which he founded in 1956, was one of the forerunners of the UFW. From the time it was founded, Itliong and other Filipino workers fought hard to have the FFLU recognized as a union. They soon received their biggest vote of support, both moral and financial, from the American Federation of Labor and Congress of Industrial Organizations (AFL-CIO), the most powerful labor group in the United States, which until that time had done little organizing among farm workers. With the help of the AFL-CIO, Itliong's union emerged as the Agricultural Workers Organizing Committee (AWOC) in 1960. Although the AWOC made some progress in bettering working conditions for its members, it did not achieve national recognition until 1965, when the strike it led against California's grape growers focused attention on the exploitation of the state's agricultural laborers.

The grape and wine industries of California depended on the labor of large groups of migrant workers who spent their life picking grapes and traveling to the next vineyard, following the crops north throughout the harvest season. Most if not all of these workers were immigrants, primarily Filipinos and Mexicans, and some of them had been picking and following the crops for 30 years. Yet working conditions were abominable, and the pay was barely a livable wage. The grape strike began when the AWOC convinced 1,000 grape workers in 3 vineyards near Thermal, California, to strike. Because the harvesting season for grapes is so short, the loss of workers even for a few weeks could have meant the loss of the crop, and the owners of the three vineyards quickly gave in to the strikers' demands for higher pay. The remaining battles were not to be won so easily.

The strike moved on to Delano, California, in September of that year. Encouraged by Itliong and his fellow organizers—who set up picket lines at the vineyards and went from field to field with bullhorns, shouting inducements to strike in both Tagalog and English—2,000 workers struck the vineyards there. At Delano, Itliong convinced Cesar Chavez, whose smaller National Farm Workers Union was made up primarily of Mexicans, to join the strike. (Chavez eventually became much better known as a labor organizer than Itliong did, and his is still the first name many people think of when they think of farm worker

Larry Dulay Itliong (front left) and Cesar Chavez (front right) led the United Farm Workers in their strike against California's grape growers, which began in 1965. Their cause received a boost when Walter Reuther (front center), president of the United Auto Workers, pledged his powerful union's support.

unions.) By the end of September, Itliong estimated, 95 percent of the grape workers in the area were on strike.

During the action, the Filipino community hall in Delano was used as the strike headquarters. The Filipino women in the community fed thousands of striking—and therefore penniless—workers while the action continued, and clothing donated to the workers by sympathizers was distributed through the community hall. A highlight of the strike was the March to Sacramento, the state capital, in March 1966. A core group of strikers—primarily Filipinos and Mexicans—marched the entire 230-mile route, and thousands of others joined them for shorter periods along the way.

The attention of the national news media and prominent politicians such as Robert Kennedy, senator from New York, soon drew public concern about the injustices suffered by California's migrant workers, and boycotts of California grapes and wine took place around the nation. As the boycotts began to affect their profit margins, the growers gradually gave in to the workers' demands for union recognition, higher wages, and better fringe benefits. The grape strike finally came to an end in 1970, when two of the largest growers, Bianco and Bruno Dispoto vineyards, signed contracts with the workers. The pressure on the grape growers had also convinced the walnut and almond growers to follow suit and sign contracts as well. By that point, Itliong's union had merged with Chavez's to form the United Farm Workers Union. Itliong, who was the UFW's second in command, eventually resigned his position because he felt the union leadership was moving too far away—both emotionally and geographically—from the workers, with whom he felt he belonged. He died in 1977, but the union he helped found is still a powerful force that represents agricultural workers throughout the United States.

The Aquinos

In the comparatively short time that they have been in this country, Filipino Americans have indeed amassed a record of considerable achievement. Yet the story of Filipino immigration to the United States also includes those who spent time in this country and then returned to the Philippines, determined to use the economic and educational opportunities that they took advantage of here to make a better life for themselves, their family, and their compatriots in the homeland. Of these, not one is so well known as Corazon Aquino, leader of the people's crusade that overthrew Marcos in 1986.

Corazon Aquino differed from most Filipinos who came to this country in that she came from an extremely wealthy and prominent family. The former Maria Corazon Cojuangco was born on January 25, 1933, in the Tarlac province of the Philippines, where the vast Cojuangco family corporation had gotten its start by milling rice and sugar. The Cojuangcos were politically well connected in addition to being rich. Corazon's father was a Filipino congressman; her grandfather, a former vice-presidential candidate; and her uncle, a senator. The young Corazon lived a sheltered childhood, attending exclusive convent schools until 1946, when her family left the war-torn Philippines for the United States. There, as in the Philippines, she attended exclusive Catholic girls' schools, first in Philadelphia, then in New York City, where she completed her college education at the College of Mount St. Vincent in a suburban section of the Bronx. Corazon returned to the Philippines to study law at the Far Eastern University in Manila, but she gave up her studies in 1954 to marry Benigno Aquino, a young Filipino politician who was also the scion of a prestigious Tarlac family.

Ninoy, as Benigno Aquino was better known, compiled a remarkable political record. He made Philippine history as the islands' youngest mayor, at age 22; youngest governor, at 29; and youngest senator, at 34. Benigno Aquino's success made him Marcos's most feared rival. By 1972, he was ready to run for the presidency, but after Marcos declared martial law he had Ninoy imprisoned on trumped-up charges of attempted murder, subversion, and weapons possession.

Ninoy spent the next seven years and seven months incarcerated in a Philippine prison. During that time Corazon was forced to become more directly involved in Philippine politics than she had ever wished to be. She spent countless hours with her husband in his cell, bringing him news of what was happening outside the prison walls and listening to his political strategies. Despite hidden cameras and listening devices, she was often able to carry written and spoken messages past the guards to his allies outside.

Although in 1977 Marcos had imposed the death sentence on Benigno Aquino, three years later he allowed Aquino to travel to the United States for a desperately needed triple bypass operation. Marcos assumed that Ninoy would never dare return so long as a death sentence hung over his head, but he underestimated his rival's determination. Although he was joined in his American exile by his wife and children and was able to secure work lecturing at universities such as Harvard and the Massachusetts Institute of Technology, Ninoy spent much of his time planning his return, despite the protestations of Corazon, who professed to be quite happy as an American housewife.

In August 1983, with Marcos in poor health and the opposition to his regime growing in strength, Aquino believed the time was right for his return. On the 21st of that month, a plane carrying Benigno Aquino landed at the airport in Manila. Soldiers boarded it almost immediately and hustled Aquino off; seconds later shots rang out and the opposition leader lay dead on the tarmac. Although subsequent investigations have never proven a definite link, it is believed by many that the hand of Ferdinand Marcos was at work in Aquino's assassination.

In mourning, Corazon Aquino returned to the nation of her birth, where her grief was shared by countless Filipinos. On the day of Ninoy's funeral, more than 1 million people lined the 80-mile route taken by his funeral cortege from Manila to the cemetery where he was buried.

Benigno Aquino's death galvanized resistance to Marcos, and massive demonstrations against his rule took place. Yet the opposition remained divided among itself on such questions as who would succeed

Ninoy and was thus unable to present a united front. The obvious choice as a leader who could unite the various factions was Corazon Aquino, but for some time the widow steadfastly resisted entreaties that she take a political role. Unable to shake the thought that she was the only one who could conclude her husband's unfinished business, Corazon Aquino finally agreed that she would run for president if Marcos allowed elections. Under pressure from the United States and world opinion to enact at least the semblance of democratic reforms, Marcos set elections for February 1986. Although not an accomplished public speaker, Corazon Aquino proved an inspirational candidate. Usually dressed in a simple yellow dress, for millions of Filipinos she became the incarnation of the opposition to Marcos and the desire for a more just and democratic society. On February 7, 1986—election day—her promises of an end to the mistreatment the Filipino people had received at the hands of Marcos inspired millions to vote for her.

Benigno Aquino's body lies on the runway following his murder at Manila International Airport on August 21, 1983.

Although Marcos had no intention of allowing the election to proceed fairly—in certain districts his soldiers intimidated voters at gunpoint, bribed others to vote for him, and even ripped up written ballots in full view of hundreds of foreign journalists—the majority of Filipinos had decided that this time election fraud would not be tolerated. Poll watchers formed human barricades to protect ballot boxes from Marcos's thugs, and government vote tabulators walked off their jobs in protest. The Philippines's Catholic bishops denounced Marcos's election tactics, and the U.S. Senate echoed their protest.

Although Marcos declared himself the winner, he failed to recognize that the people were no longer willing to endure his program of corruption, deceit, and intimidation. Hundreds of thousands of Filipinos took to the streets in protest. Even two of Marcos's seemingly most loyal deputies defected to the opposition. Juan Ponce Enrile, the country's defense minister, and Lieutenant General Fidel Ramos, the deputy chief of the armed forces, declared Aquino to be the election's true winner and barricaded themselves, with their troops, inside two military camps. In Manila, tens of thousands of Filipinos, many clad in yellow or carrying yellow flowers, placed their unprotected bodies between the rebels and the guns of the soldiers still loyal to Marcos. Aquino had herself inaugurated as presi-

When Marcos called out tanks and troops to put down the insurrection led by a former general and defense minister, thousands of Filipinos lined the streets of Manila to impede their progress.

Former first lady Imelda Marcos's shoe collection has become the symbol of the profligate excess of her husband's despotic regime.

dent, and Marcos accepted the United States's offer for asylum in Hawaii. The Malacanang Palace, where he and his family had lived in opulent excess at the expense of the Filipino people, was thrown open to the public, who gaped in wonder at the riches that had been left behind, including the more than 3,000 pairs of shoes that filled First Lady Imelda Marcos's enormous closets.

Despite her popularity, Corazon Aquino has not been able to solve all of the Philippines's problems. Poverty remains widespread, and it will take years for the economy to recover from the depredations of the Marcos era. Communist rebels continue to enjoy success in the countryside, where the peasants still suffer from inequitable land distribution. Corruption remains a virtually accepted by-product of the political process, and congressional elections in the late 1980s were marred by violence and political assassinations. Filipino immigrants continue to come to the United States in large numbers. Among those who have made their new homes here are Ferdinand and Imelda Marcos and many of their cronies and henchmen. Yet under Aquino's leadership the Philippines has made great strides as well. Perhaps the most noteworthy accomplishment has been the ratification of a new democratic constitution, which along with Aquino's leadership seems to offer Filipinos the hope of a brighter future.

Next to Mexican Americans, Filipino Americans are the fastest growing immigrant group in the United States.

FILIPINO AMERICANS TODAY

I n 1980 the U.S. Census Bureau reported that there were 774,652 Filipinos in the United States. They settled in each of the nation's 50 states and constituted less than 1 percent of the U.S. population. At least half the Filipino Americans living in the United States today were born in the Philippines, and their numbers continue to grow every year. More than 40,000 Filipinos have immigrated to this country each year since 1980; in 1986 that number topped 50,000. By 1990 the number of Filipino Americans in the United States will almost certainly exceed 1 million.

The number of Filipinos allowed into the United States under the current immigration quota system is small compared to the number who are trying to gain entrance. The U.S. State Department's Bureau of Consular Affairs reports that depending on the quota category, applications are backed up to the early 1980s and, in one case, to 1976, which means that there can be as long as a 10-year wait to immigrate to the United States.

The high total of Filipino immigrants in 1986—the year that Aquino became president of the Philippines—shows that the desire to come to the United States has not lessened under the new government. Lack of economic opportunity in the Philippines remains the primary motivating force for emigration. With a huge foreign debt and a sluggish national economy, the Philippines simply cannot offer its citizens the chance to live the good life that can be had in this country. Although the educated Filipinos who constitute the bulk of the new immigrants are aware that their talents are badly needed at home, the comparative riches to be earned in the United States are too great a temptation for them to resist.

Where They Live

Today, Filipino Americans still live mainly in the far western United States. In 1980, California alone was home to 357,492 of them, and Hawaii claimed another 133,940. In California, Filipinos are the largest Asian population group. Most live in the state's urban areas, particularly in the San Francisco–Oakland, Los Angeles–Long Beach, San Diego, Stockton, San Jose, and Salinas-Monterey areas.

This pattern of mostly urban living is repeated in other states. The new generation of immigrants is settling in cities, where their professional and technical skills are appreciated. Nationwide, the 1980 census found that more than 90 percent of Filipino Americans lived in metropolitan areas. In this regard, they are quite unlike their earlier counterparts, who lived mostly in rural areas, where they earned their living by engaging in semiskilled agricultural work.

Three cities have very dense Filipino-American populations. In 1980, almost 100,000 Filipino Americans lived in metropolitan Honolulu, Hawaii, and similar numbers were found in the San Francisco and Los Angeles areas. Other major cities with large Filipino-American populations include Chicago, with 41,283, and New York City, with 23,810.

Brain Gain

Since 1965, the Philippines has been the number one foreign source of engineers, physicians, and technical workers for the United States. The eagerness of its professionals to emigrate has caused many problems for the Philippines, as it has resulted in that nation losing many of its smartest and most ambitious citizens, but the brain drain has benefited the United States. The relatively high quality of professional education in the Philippines, much of it either established by the United States or based on American models, has allowed it to provide this country with a much-needed supply of professional workers.

One example of this is in the medical field. In the late 1960s and early 1970s, the United States experienced a shortage of doctors. This was in part the result of an increased demand for medical services that resulted from the 1965 establishment of Medicaid, government-supported health care for the poor, and Medicare, health assistance for the elderly. As a result, hospitals began to look overseas to fill their need for doctors. Seventy-five thousand foreign doctors came to the United States between 1965 and 1974, either to stay permanently or to practice here temporarily, and Filipino doctors—with their careful training in American medical techniques back home—were the largest national group among them. By 1976, when the United States suspended the special laws designed to bring foreign doctors to this country, there were already 9,000 Filipino doctors practicing here—40 percent of the worldwide total of Filipino physicians. In general, immigrant Filipino doctors have been less able to get the high-paying, comfortable positions attained by many American-born physicians and therefore have become an important medical resource for the poorer

Many of the new wave of Filipino immigrants are doctors. Enrique Araneta is a psychiatrist who specializes in the treatment of Vietnam veterans for posttraumatic stress disorder.

Americans who live in our inner cities and in rural areas.

Nursing has also been a very common profession for Filipino Americans. Under U.S. immigration laws, nurses qualify for entrance as the kind of technical workers in demand here. Because of the recent nursing shortage, they are easily able to get their certification to practice here, unlike doctors, pharmacists, and other professionals. During the 1970s, approximately one-fifth of all the men and women graduated from Philippine nursing schools immigrated to the United States—about 400 of them a year. Today, U.S. hospitals, especially those in the inner cities, are still desperately in need of nurses, and the Philippines continues to supply many of them.

Nursing aside, obtaining licensing has been a major problem for Filipino professionals who have immigrated to the United States. The problem is made doubly complicated because the individual states, rather than the federal government, are responsible for licensing. The states have different rules and requirements for receiving licenses, and some of these rules make things difficult for immigrants. For example, some states require that a licensed professional be a citizen or have filed intent to become one. Others require some experience in this country as a practitioner before a license is issued. For that reason, many Filipino doctors and dentists end up working for years as technicians before they can obtain the proper credentials for licensing. Others work at even lower paying jobs. H. Brett Melendy, who chronicled the history of Filipino Americans in his book *Asians in America*, writes of one Filipino doctor who came here in 1970 with 16 years of medical experience in the Philippines. Before getting his license, he worked first as a janitor and then finally as a butcher. He did not tell his new employers that he was a doctor, but they were quite impressed with his work anyway. As he told Melendy, "They thought I was very good at separating the meat from the bone."

Hope for the Future

Despite the many hardships and setbacks they have endured, Filipino Americans are doing very well as a group. Their success derives from both their professional skills and their ambition. Next to Japanese Americans, in 1980 Filipino Americans had the lowest unemployment rate of any ethnic group, including American whites. In that year, 80 percent of working Filipino Americans were employed in the private sector, and many worked in high-paying fields: 33.3 percent had technical or service-related jobs, and 25.1 percent held managerial or professional positions. At the time the 1980 census was conducted, their average family income was higher than that of all other ethnic groups in the United States except Japanese Americans and East Indian Americans.

Economic success has not come at the expense of group cohesiveness. It has been said that whenever two Filipinos get together, they form a club, and whenever three get together, they form a community. Since the days of the Sociedad de Beneficencia de los Hispano Filipinos de Nuevo Orleans in the 1870s, Filipino Americans have been forming societies, both for the purposes of socialization and for their mutual benefit. Filipino Americans today maintain a large number of cultural, social, and benevolent societies, which aim to preserve Filipino culture and to help recent arrivals become established. A recent count found more than 400 of these organizations in California alone.

Contemporary Filipino Americans also look after their own community in other ways. For example, in the 1970s, a group of younger Filipinos organized themselves to help aging Filipino farm workers live a comfortable old age. Among their actions was the founding of the Paulo Agbayani Retirement Village near Delano, California, which provides housing and health care for the older generation who did so much to prepare the way for those who came later. The senior citizens community was named after an early Filipino labor organizer.

In addition to their many clubs and social organizations, the Filipino-American press also enables immigrants and their descendants to stay in touch with events in the old country and other immigrant communities. Filipino Americans have published newspapers and newsletters since their earliest days in the

Max Fabella edits the Filipiniana, *a newspaper that serves the Filipino community of northeast Florida.*

United States. Most of the publications have been short lived, apearing for a few years and then ceasing for lack of staffing or money. Yet others always arise to take their place. The number of Filipino-American publications is not officially tracked by any organization, making an accurate total difficult to come by. The last published account of the Filipino-American press was an article in *Journalism Quarterly*, in 1977. The author, Donn Hart, a professor at Northern Illinois University, found a total of 19 newspapers, 8 newsletters, and 1 magazine published by and for Filipino Americans. All were written in English, the common language of all Filipino ethnic groups, although some also had a few articles in Tagalog. Today, as in the past, Filipino-American publications concentrate on the activities of the many Filipino-American organizations, including meetings and elections; the successes of various Filipino-American businesspeople, politicians, and other professionals; social events such as weddings and baptisms; and the visits of prominent Filipinos to the United States. They also cover legal issues that affect their readers, such as licensing requirements and immigration and visa regulations. Although they cover politics in the Philippines to some extent, much of this coverage is left to the mainstream press. The Filipino-American community can look forward to a bright future. With their dedication to education, to family, and to helping others within their community, they seem to have hit on a formula for success in America. As their numbers continue to grow at the current fast pace, they are likely to develop more political power in the cities where they are concentrated, and one day soon it will be impossible for anyone to speak of them as a forgotten minority.

Only one factor is likely to change their present course: the political situation in the Philippines. For

A Filipino-American barber outside his Honolulu shop in 1985. The struggle of the older generation of Filipino Americans made it easier for the immigrants who followed to succeed.

Adjusting to life in America: Two Filipino-American children romp on their playroom floor while watching Saturday-morning cartoons.

although the United States benefits by having highly educated Filipinos come to live here, the Philippines suffers by their loss. If Corazon Aquino and her successors as president can rejuvenate the Philippine economy and restore hope to the thousands planning to leave the country, the brain drain from the Philippines could stop, and the great wave of Filipino immigration might be reduced to a trickle. Yet although many Filipinos and Filipino Americans hope that real and lasting change will come to the Philippines, no one is counting on it happening in the near future. Whatever the coming years bring, the United States will continue to be a haven for the Philippines's economic and political exiles, a place where, despite their minority status, they can find people that speak their language and appreciate the job skills they have to offer. Filipinos have long recognized the United States as a special land; as their numbers here grow, Filipino Americans are sure to win increased recognition as a special people.

FURTHER READING

Bulosan, Carlos. *America is in the Heart: A Personal History.* Seattle: University of Washington Press, 1973.

Chua-Eoan, Howard. *Corazon Aquino.* New York: Chelsea House, 1988.

Cordova, Fred. *Filipinos, Forgotten Asian Americans: A Pictorial Essay, 1763-circa 1963.* Dubuque, IA: Kendall/Hunt Publishing, 1983.

Costa, Horacio de la, ed. *Readings in Philippine History.* Manila: Bookmark, 1965.

Crouchett, Lorraine Jacobs. *Filipinos in California: From the Days of the Galleons to the Present.* El Cerrito, CA: Downey Place, 1982.

DeWitt, Howard A. *Anti-Filipino Movements in California: A History, Bibliography, and Study Guide.* San Francisco: R & E Research Publishers, 1976.

Grunder, Garel A., and William E. Livezey. *The Philippines and the United States.* Norman: University of Oklahoma Press, 1951.

Komisar, Lucy. *Corazon Aquino: The Story of a Revolution.* New York: Braziller, 1987.

Melendy, Howard Brett. *Asians in America: Filipinos, Koreans and East Indians.* New York: Hippocrene Books, 1981.

Nelson, Raymond. *The Philippines.* New York: Walker & Company, 1968.

Reimers, David M. *Still the Golden Door: The Third World Comes to America.* New York: Columbia University Press, 1985.

Shalom, Stephen Rosskamm. *The United States and the Philippines: A Study of Neocolonialism. Studies in Political Economy.* Philadelphia: Institute for the Study of Human Issues, 1981.

Slack, Gordy. *Ferdinand Marcos.* New York: Chelsea House, 1988.

INDEX

PICTURE CREDITS

JENNIFER STERN is a free-lance writer living in New York City. She received a B.A. in English from Dartmouth College and an M.A. in urban planning from Hunter College. She has published articles in *Planning* and *Rolling Stone* and is a contributing editor for *City Limits* and *Video Review.*

DANIEL PATRICK MOYNIHAN is the senior United States senator from New York. He is also the only person in American history to serve in the cabinets or subcabinets of four successive presidents—Kennedy, Johnson, Nixon, and Ford. Formerly a professor of government at Harvard University, he has written and edited many books, including *Beyond the Melting Pot, Ethnicity: Theory and Experience* (both with Nathan Glazer), *Loyalties,* and *Family and Nation.*